Starting Over,

One Cake at a Time

a&b

Starting Over, One Cake at a Time

GESINE BULLOCK-PRADO

First published in Great Britain in 2011 by
Allison & Busby Limited
13 Charlotte Mews
London, W1T 4EJ
www.allisonandbusby.com

Copyright © 2009 by GESINE BULLOCK-PRADO

The moral right of the author has been asserted.

*The names of some people have been changed in order to
protect their privacy.*

A CIP catalogue record for this book is available from
the British Library.

First published in the US in 2009.

10 9 8 7 6 5 4 3 2 1

ISBN 978-0-7490-0863-5

Typeset in 10.5/17 pt Sabon by
Allison & Busby Ltd.

Paper used in this publication is from sustainably managed sources.
All of the wood used is procured from legal sources and is fully traceable.
The producing mill uses schemes such as ISO 14001
to monitor environmental impact.

Printed and bound in the UK by
CPI Mackays, Chatham ME5 8TD

Für Mutti

Contents

Recipes

Prologue

The Devil in St. Nick

I SAW THE DEVIL AT AGE THREE and he gave me chocolate. It changed my life forever.

On the evening of December 6th, 1973, in Salzburg, Austria, something stood on the landing just outside the door of our Schillerstrasse apartment, let loose an agonising moan, and rattled a ghastly chorus of heavy chains. My mother whooped in delight and invited me to open the door.

'Sina! Mach auf!'

I was no stranger to this kind of perversely dark German childhood experience. My first storybook, *Struwwelpeter*, told such heartwarming tales as 'The

Story of the Thumb Sucker' in which a naughty boy gets his thumbs cut off when he persists in that odious habit. Illustrations included. Or the story of the rascal Kaspar who, upon proclaiming he will no longer eat his soup, wastes away and dies, again accompanied by beautifully detailed artwork. And, there's Pauline who insists on playing with matches. She certainly deserves to be consumed by those bright orange flames that take her to a fiery death. These children were not alone in their misdeeds; I myself was an avid nail biter. And, as my cousin Suzanne liked to remind me hourly, I once pooped on the Persian rug in the foyer. I was a toddler. What did I know?

But even worse, in the estimation of my majestically gorgeous and perpetually svelte mother, I was sugar obsessed. I was both grotesquely undisciplined and a potential fatty, effortlessly breaching two cardinal sins in my mother's endless ledger of unforgivable venialities. To hide my growing addiction I became a candy thief, taking primarily from the 'secret' sweets drawer in my aunt's credenza and sometimes from my friend Katya's bedside table stash. It was for these ugly crimes that I had been anticipating an untimely end similar to those of Kaspar, Pauline, and that poor thumb-sucking boy. And now the devil had come to my door; my mother had apparently subcontracted her daughter's grisly disposal.

I wasn't going to help invite death in. My sister, five

years older, wiser, and intent on setting unspeakable terrors upon me, opened the door herself. She was acquainted with our dark caller; she'd experienced him both as jolly Santa in America and as his cranky German alter ego, Saint Nikolaus. Either way, the outcome was usually pretty good for her on both sides of the Atlantic. We had dual natures ourselves; equal parts German and American, a bit of both our mother and our father. Our German mother, a professional opera singer, carted us to Europe while she toured, and our Alabama-born father kept the stateside fires burning in Virginia, toiling inside the rings of the Pentagon.

My sister opened the door just in time for us to spy a gruesome creature layered in chains, a filthy burlap sack strapped to his back and a leather collar cinched about his pockmarked neck. Attached to the collar was a leash, and as I followed the length of rope to the hand that grasped the lead, I beheld what appeared to be the devil himself. Our visiting demon was lank and grey-bearded, draped head to toe in sooty red velvet robes and sporting an impractically tall pointed hat. He left two matching velvet stockings leaning against the door jamb, brimming with chocolates bearing his likeness and countless other sweets. Once he and his henchman were safely out of child-snatching range, I braved the open hallway to grab the loot.

But before I could marvel at the bounty, I stood to

face our benefactor. If I was going to take his offering, I felt obliged to overcome my fear and acknowledge his generosity by looking him straight in the eye, devil or not. He had gone through all the trouble of finding us. He'd probably checked in Virginia first. And then he'd have tracked us to Germany and followed the trail to Austria. And he could have left us coal. But he gave us chocolate. All of this and he was going to leave it at our door without taking credit for his trouble and kindness.

'Grüß Gott, Herr Teufel. Vielen dank.'

He scoffed at my greeting, literally translated, 'Greet God, Mr. Devil. Many thanks.'

'Grüß Gott, Ferkel.' Little piglet, he called me a little piglet. Sure, it was a term of endearment, but I was anything but a little piglet. He knew that.

And so it followed that he was anything but a devil. In fact, he was a misunderstood angel; he was the great Saint Nikolaus accompanied by his festering sidekick Krampus. And to put the final dusting of lustre on this confectionary miracle, my mother allowed us unlimited access to the contents of our velvet stockings.

I had less spectacular run-ins with confections while in Europe that I remember in an equal amount of detail: my fourth birthday cake, rimmed with marzipan clown heads and filled with almond cake and cream; the After Eight mints hidden in the credenza of the study in my aunt's home in Bergen,

Germany, top drawer of the middle row, behind the Christmas napkins; the stockpile of gummi bears in my grandmother's handbag, which she doled out as bribery to keep me walking on the harsh cobblestone streets of Nürnberg during shopping expeditions. She herself kept a bar of the blackest bittersweet chocolate to bolster her own shopping spirits.

Martha, our American nanny, conjured slim packages of lemon cream-filled wafers from the pockets of her prairie skirts to coax me along on our daily visit to see my mother during her matinee performance. We crossed the river Salzach on the footbridge that connects the old Salzburg to the new. I portioned each wafer perfectly to coincide with our walk to the Landestheater, one tiny nibble to every ten footfalls on the narrow cobblestone streets. Once we reached the metal stairs that clung to the side of the building and led to the stage door, I would modulate my bites to coincide with the ring of every fourth step. I lifted my knees high and let my foot land squarely on the tread so that the sonorous metal ring would vibrate through my body and add more drama to the crunch of each bite.

Inside, the backstage hallways teemed with men in period costume, their britches open exposing girdles buckling from strain. Sweat streaked their heavily pancaked faces and loosened the glue holding their handlebar moustaches fast. Martha would usher me hastily past my mother's empty dressing room and through a side door into the theatre, where I would slip into an empty seat for my afternoon nap. I might wake to see her mid-belly dance, or engaging in a lusty kiss or suffering a consumptive death. Once, I woke during a rehearsal of *Carmen* to see my sister among the gypsy children on stage, dramatically lunging for prop coins being thrown her way. The director invited us both to join a slew of other vagabonds to round out the cast, but I suffered from painful shyness and a general distrust of strangers. My sister had no such problems and took to the stage with hammy delight. At home, she emptied her pockets on her bed and revealed that the fake lucre she was scooping up on stage was in fact beautifully wrapped chocolates. Had I only known the rewards awaiting me, I might have conquered my timidity. I had, after all, faced a devil for chocolate only to find that I was in the presence of a saint. And in the end it was the example of unlikely angels and the power of confections that led me on a sweet path to happiness and grace in my adult life.

Chapter One

The Witching Hour

3 a.m.

I WAKE UP AT THE WITCHING HOUR. 3:30 a.m. According to folklore, it's the very moment when witches, demons, and ghosts are at their most potent. It's also when most bakers roll their flour-logged bodies out of bed.

My husband, Ray, sleeps through my alarm. I can't look at him, sleeping or awake, without getting a little weak in the knees. He's more handsome now than he was ten years ago when we first met in Hollywood, home to the prettiest boys and girls on the planet. My job was to develop films for those beautiful people. It was a miracle that I could find anyone attractive, I was so anaesthetised by the constant parade of bleached smiles and spray-on tans. But there he was, sitting across from me at a conference table at a big studio meeting, an honest-to-god Man, handsome as all get out. And smart. And funny. And not an actor. An illustrator for film, in fact. An employed artist and a grown-up, something in rare supply in Los Angeles among the insecure, fame-hungry hordes of beefcake.

I sit up. Stretch. The dogs wake long enough to yawn and deliver a few sloppy kisses, and then all three jump into my still-warm side of the bed, burrow under the covers, and snuggle up to Ray.

I take a bath, brush my teeth, and pull back my hair. For this very brief moment I see what's become of my black mane. I'm in possession of Crystal Gayle-like, snake-handling, ankle-skimming hippie hair. Only a few years ago I'd drop major cash to get it permanently and perversely straight. To look at it now, you'd think I'd been scheduling regular appointments with a live power outlet.

I pad naked down the stairs, wanting so much to take a detour to the kitchen to make coffee but head instead to the laundry room and rummage for something clean to wear. I don't care that our clothes never make it from the intertwined dance of the dryer to the smooth folds of the dresser drawers anymore. If it's clean and comfortable, I'll pull it on.

Today I'm sporting a dryer-culled ensemble

consisting of an ancient Al 'Big Daddy' Roth T-shirt emblazoned with his signature hot-rod-straddling rat caricature flipping the bird. It's unbelievably soft, manhandled by some grizzled biker into buttery suppleness and then graciously sold to me on eBay. At the moment, it's both graphically offensive and soon to be encrusted with chocolate. It also sets off my growing collection of knife and burn wounds to great effect. My pants are ratty blue cords with a malfunctioning zipper circa 1978. They are number one on my queue of pants to wear to work, being both roomy in the thigh and so fantastically high-waisted that they don't require a belt. My clogs are encrusted in flour and my socks don't match. If my mother were alive, she'd be horrified that I'd half-consciously chosen this getup. She was, after all, the only mother at my elementary school who routinely wore leather pants and high heels. But if she knew my purpose, she'd forgive me any sartorial sin. She may have been a well-respected opera diva and an outrageously sexy and fashionable woman, but she was also our family's resident master baker.

I was once a beautifully dressed woman. I have storage bins, tucked away in the attic of our barn, filled with 'grown-up' gear – smart pantsuits and death-defying heels, leather briefcases and tailored overcoats. I can't bring myself to give the stuff away; I dragged every stitch from LA to rural Vermont. My beef was never with the clothes I had to wear to work in Hollywood, it was with Hollywood itself. So I keep them because they were innocent bystanders in my past misery as a cog in the wheel of the entertainment industry. And many of them are from my sister, better known as 'Sand-me-downs'. Luxurious, couture bits of fashion she gets for free for being a movie star. Every few months she weeds through her closet and sets aside things she's never worn and will never wear. And since she's a loving and generous big sister, she sends me the prime nuggets. So they have sentimental value as well.

Unlike me, my sister found her calling early in life. Sandy's also gifted genetically. She inherited my mother's razor-sharp jaw and mile-high cheekbones. Her thick black wavy hair came from our father, but she blessedly missed that family's predilection to start greying as teenagers. She pulled the dimple in her chin from a source so distant that no one in living memory has possessed one, and her sweet nose comes from Germany by way of my grandfather Meyer. Her wit and winning personality surely come from the Bullocks; both our father and Aunt Luddy can spin a yarn and charm the pants off anyone. Her talent could have come from either side, artistry bursting from our DNA at every angle. My sister was also blessed with great humility and cultivated a habit of downplaying her attributes and rerouting any and all attention or praise on me. Usually she does this in my absence. She'll meet someone and feel the need to tell him or her I am brilliant. And she tells them I am beautiful and tall.

In the face of someone as beautiful as my sister, they come to think that I must be an otherworldly beauty if she describes me that way. Bless her; I think she really thinks all these wonderful things of me.

To be honest, I'm bright but not brilliant. Bookish and being a smart-ass really don't add up to genius, though I wish they did. And the words most often used to describe me physically – exotic or striking or stunning – all translate to tall, pretty girl with black hair and a prominent nose. On more than one occasion, someone has pointed at me as evidence that my sister has had 'work done'. I'm the 'before' to her 'after'. But more often, I'm asked why it is that I don't look more like her, to which I reply, 'So sorry to disappoint you, you ass.'

She also forgets to add to her long list of superlatives for me that I am a socially retarded misanthrope, awkward on the best of occasions and completely witless and offensive on the worst. So my chosen profession, one in which I am required to work behind closed doors in the darkest hours of the morning with very little contact with other humans, is quite fitting.

On this black morning, dressed in 'baker's casual' with my still-wet hair in a sloppy ponytail, I'm searching for my car keys and I look out the kitchen window to see where the moon hangs. If it's just above our first ridge of pine, lighting my path to the barn door, I'm making good time. Any hint of daybreak and I'm screwed. In the winter, the path is a slippery white corridor. Pearly walls reaching up to our chins, small arterial tunnels dug by the dogs breaking off from the main throughway and leading into places unknown.

In the summer, moonlight permitting, I greet the toads that linger at the side door, tales of soggy midnight rainstorms and dewy grass clinging to their skin. Apple green luna moths, as big as my palm, loiter on the glass of the kitchen door. I see their fuzzy bellies first and carefully open the door to admire their handsome wings before they fly away.

My headlights flood the ghostly dark dirt roads twisting from our house to the paved street that leads to Montpelier. I have fifteen minutes of uncorrupted driving ahead of me. Not one luxury car cutting me off in the narrow canyons of the Hollywood Hills. Not a single Harley shattering my solitude on Sunset Boulevard. No road rage, no cell phones, no fake tits or tans, no prestige handbags, no billboards, no stoplights, no braking, no traffic, no nothing. Welcome to Vermont. Just heaven.

Golden Eggs

I HAVE THOUSANDS of great recipes but only one magic recipe. It's vanilla cake, really just an ordinary yellow cake. Plain old humdrum yellow cake. Big deal. So where's the magic?

Made simply, with pure vanilla extract and vanilla beans, this cake is hands-down the best thing ever. It's moist and dense but still effortlessly springy. The vanilla lives deep in this batter; it permeates every molecule of butter and imparts a richness of flavour that trumps every other yellow cake out there.

But you can take out the vanilla and still make grown men cry. Add lemon extract and fresh blueberries and you've just made a groundbreaking muffin. Add sour cherries and orange extract, sprinkle a buttery streusel on top before baking, and you've made every other coffee cake obsolete.

But if you really want to mess with people, if you want to make something that is both confusing and outrageously delicious, make a Golden Egg.

I created the Golden Egg for Easter. I make hot cross buns too, but I wanted to offer something else.

Something special. I consulted my magic recipe. And I remembered reading about a technique that made ordinary cake taste like doughnuts, without all the deep-frying. That's pretty special.

I make Golden Eggs year-round now; they're not just for Easter anymore. And they are coveted as if they were indeed genuine 14-carat gold.

MAKES 12 EGGS OR ABOUT 12 MUFFIN-SIZED CAKES

For the cake
Nonstick baking spray
3 cups all-purpose flour
1 tablespoon baking powder
1 teaspoon salt
1 teaspoon nutmeg
½ pound (2 sticks) unsalted butter, at room temperature
2 cups sugar
5 large eggs, at room temperature
1 teaspoon vanilla extract
1¼ cups nonfat buttermilk

For dipping the eggs
8 tablespoons (1 stick) unsalted butter, melted
1 cup sugar and 1 teaspoon cinnamon mixed together in a small shallow bowl

Preheat the oven to 325°F/170°C. Spray your moulds with nonstick spray. (I, obviously, use egg-shaped moulds. You can use a muffin pan or any other small baking moulds.)

Sift together the flour, baking powder, salt, and nutmeg. Set aside.

In an electric mixer fitted with either the paddle or the whisk attachment, whip the butter and sugar together until light and fluffy. This can take up to 10 minutes, depending on the temperature of your butter. As you're whipping away, stop and scrape down the sides of the bowl to make sure all the butter is incorporated into the sugar. You can't make magic without a lot of patience. So keep whipping and keep scraping.

Add the eggs one at a time, whipping after each one until the egg is fully incorporated into the batter. Scrape down the bowl every now and again as well. Add the vanilla.

Once all the eggs are incorporated, alternate adding the flour mixture and the buttermilk, mixing slowly. After they are well incorporated but not overbeaten, take a rubber spatula and fold the batter a few times to make sure everything is evenly distributed and the batter is smooth.

Distribute the batter into your moulds, filling each cavity a little less than halfway. Bake for about

15 minutes. Baking time varies depending on the size of your mould, so check for a very light golden brown colour and make sure the cake springs back when you touch it.

Unmould your little cakes and while they are still warm, dunk them quickly in the melted butter, then dredge them in the cinnamon and sugar. One warning: people are going to call you a stinking liar. They will not believe that these precious morsels aren't fried like a doughnut. But that's the cost of making magic.

Chapter Two

To Thine Own Baking Self Be True

4 a.m.

GETTING CLOSER TO TOWN, small farms give way to neat rows of wood-clad Cape Cods, built in the 1800s, some kept as fastidiously now as they were back then by their Dutch builders. Others are a little the worse for wear, Tibetan prayer flags spanning the front porches and marking the homes as communal breeding grounds for modern-day hippies. My shop is just around the corner, as you enter the city limits of Montpelier in a neighbourhood we call the 'Meadow'. Our sign jumps out first, a gold owl set against a black background. My mother never got to see my life revolution from Hollywood cog to baker, but she's always with me. Since she was a young girl her nickname had been Eule, owl in German. So our store logo, our protector and my totem, is a horned owl that Ray hand-drew on a scrap of paper, inspired by our new life and by her memory.

We're across from Terry Shannon's convenience store, the eponymously named Meadow Mart, and still a few blocks away from the city centre that houses the administrative works of the state of Vermont, a gold-domed capitol building, the DMV, a post office, five locally owned pizza joints, and two streets: State and Main. This is Montpelier, Vermont, population 8,035, the smallest state capital in the United States and the only one without a McDonald's.

I unlock the front door to my pastry shop; it's still black outside. Terry's is shuttered, a Miller Light sign glowing in the front picture window. Only a few times a year is there evidence that someone else has been up in the wee hours of the morning. A local legend, the Valentines Phantom, plasters thousands of 8½ × 11 colour photocopies of big juicy hearts all over town. Every year on February 14th the front of our store is beautifully festooned, top to bottom, with a riot of red. I take it as a matter of greedy pride that we get the most hearts. I've counted. Or on December 13th, Santa Lucia Day, there may be a blazing lantern sitting on the front stoop, left by our resident saint, Larry, to bring me light at the darkest and coldest time of the year. In return, I make him cardamom-infused Saint Lucia buns.

I push open the front door and enter at a full sprint. I have thirty seconds from the front of the shop to the alarm panel to stop the ominous beeping. Surfing across the ancient pine planks that run the length of the store, shimmying past the pastry case with index finger at the ready, I punch in the code with twenty seconds to spare.

I take a deep breath, blood pumping, and turn reverently to the tall metal repository that contains inky black beans, on the right side decaffeinated and on the left, rocket fuel. As the coffee brews, I stand a while and take in that opulent smell of freshly ground beans. How could I have dismissed the smell as a child? There's so much now that I savour that would have repulsed me as a kid. Like the aroma of yeast, the scent that greets me when I slide open the glass doors of the pastry case and pull out trays of croissants that have been resting overnight, the yeast slowly blooming and coming to life so that when I arrive at 4 a.m., they are plump and aching for the blast of a hot oven. Balancing sheet pans loaded with plain, chocolate, raspberry, almond, and savoury croissants, I kick open the door to the kitchen and power up the huge convection double ovens, 400 degrees for the top and 300 for the bottom. The fans come to life and fill the room with a constant low moan that continues until we close at 5 p.m.

I pray at the altar of the two great comestible goddesses, pastry and coffee. And while I have taken the veil as a servant of the almighty baked good, devoting my life to unearthing her secrets and guarding the sanctity of butter, sugar, and flour, I am no less in awe of the great mysteries of her holiness, java. As a matter of fact, I have only two truisms that I apply to humanity. Never trust anyone who drives an Astro van. And never trust anyone who doesn't drink beer or coffee unless they have a doctor's note.

My German grandmother, Omi, was a Grand Master in the art of the brew. At three o'clock, the sacred hour of *kaffee und kuchen* (cake and coffee), she would set about carefully rinsing out her paper-thin porcelain coffee decanter with blistering-hot water. She measured the whole beans precisely and ground them to perfect consistency in her tiny tabletop grinder. She set the water to boil and poured a steady stream over the resting beans, patiently, so that every ground was saturated with scalding water and contributed to the chocolate brown elixir that dripped from the coffee filter. Ray has taken up the mantle of Coffee Guru and can extract the most beautiful essence from a bean using one of the most complicated pieces of engineering I've ever been terrified of, the professional fully manual espresso machine. I respect his rectory of coffee and don't get near the espresso station, just as he respects my dominion over the ovens and all things pastry. But I won't be denied this ritual, the simple act of slowly dripping water over ground bean. And I need a gentle caffeinated push into wakefulness to aid me in my very long day of communing with butter and sugar.

In my former life, I'd still be asleep at this hour. I'd eventually roll out of bed around seven and drive through an endless landscape of graffitied concrete, sleazy billboards, and row after row of McMansions. Drag myself into the gym chock full of out-of-work starlets and fuel myself with dread at the thought of facing another soul-sucking day in Hollywood. Get to the office by nine. Work a full eight hours putting together the infinite pieces that get movies made, fielding thousands of calls from faceless humans, all of them swearing to be in possession of the perfect script and wouldn't Sandy be just perfect in it. And I'd come home feeling empty and useless.

I first arrived in LA, just out of college, to hang out with my sister and go to law school. Sandy got ridiculously famous by my second year there. I was driving to class, listening to mindless drive-time radio. The DJs were babbling; I was tailgating and futzing with the lid to my coffee. They were chatting for what seemed to be an eternity about this adorable girl in this cute romantic comedy their girlfriends had dragged them to and they ended up liking the movie and loving the actress in it. And then I caught on. Holy shit! They were talking about *While You Were Sleeping*. They were talking about Sandy! I became privy to these kinds of conversations all over the place – in line for coffee, at the dentist, at the dog park. At first I was delighted that she had made such a rousing success, but pretty quickly it got creepy.

I'd get home and find the answering machine full.

Messages from hundreds of fixated strangers who took the obsessive time to track down the unlisted number of a woman they didn't know, whom they had seen play a fictitious character in their local Cineplex and for whom they suddenly had a deep and meaningful attachment. Some messages were full of longing and despair. Some were eerily casual and familiar. Others were thick with menace and confusion, from poor souls who should have been heavily medicated and hospitalised, internal voices commanding them to find this woman and bring her home. But they all contained a sense of ownership, as if they'd seen a product advertised in a catalogue and were putting in their order: I saw it, I want it, I deserve it, and it's mine.

About the same time, I graduated from law school, passed the bar, and went on exactly two interviews at law firms.

'Miss Bullock, our firm is dedicated to boring the hell out of you and ensuring you have no life. Pray at the altar of billable hours!'

Comparatively, Hollywood was looking positively alluring. And as luck would have it, my sister was starting up a production company. It took me a nanosecond to say, 'Sign me up!' We were going to make movies, me armed with my nebbish book smarts to look over contracts and nitpick over inaccuracies in historical biopics. And Sandy had her boundless creative energy. I'd also be able to keep an eye out for those crazies who were calling her and she'd be able to boss around her little sister. The work wasn't particularly fulfilling, but I hadn't taken much time to figure out what would be. So for the time being it was a win-win situation. And I met Ray.

At our newly minted company, I'd get as many calls from stalkers as I got from studio executives. I had two piles on my desk. On the one side, a tidy mountain of scripts and contracts. And on the other, a freakish cumulus of creepy fan letters and items I'm reluctant to label as presents because they were really more like pagan offerings: collages composed of human hair and photos torn from trade magazines, a box of Halloween candy and razor blades. Once we got a proposal of marriage accompanied by a dozen roses and a live Dalmatian puppy. Every week I'd bundle up the freak show and ship it off to the police for cataloguing.

I read abominable scripts, lifeless books, and uninspired pitches in the morning. In the afternoon I'd have meetings with writers, studio executives, and producers in our upstairs conference room, wherein I devoted the hours between three and five trying my damnedest not to scream bloody murder whenever I heard the words *cute, quirky,* and *romantic comedy.*

And my friends, they started to call to 'do' lunch, to read their scripts, to hear their ideas, to confirm a bit of gossip. No big deal, really. Even an ex had something to sell, shamelessly sidestepping that little piece of our history where he stomped my heart to bits. After a few months, it dawned on me that I had stopped being a confidante and had become a contact. They had an 'in' and it was me. And every lunch, every dinner party, had become an opportunity to kiss my ass and sell me ideas. I'd never felt so lonely.

Every once in a while, an actual movie production would break out in between all the schmoozing. And by a movie production, I mean sitting on a set for two months waiting for something to happen.

But I had Sandy, and eventually I had Ray. So I had a buffer of comfort that tended to dull the pervasive ick that was work. And there were private jets and improbably luxurious European trips that Ray and I enjoyed as Sandy's tiny entourage on film press tours. She spent the entire day working, spruced up within an inch of her life and answering the same five questions from reporters every day for two weeks while Ray and I gallivanted around ancient Rome in a hired car, took long, wine-soaked lunches at the Café Marly overlooking the glass Egyptian pyramid of the Louvre in Gay Paree, and ate bouillabaisse on the beach at Cannes. So as you can see, it wasn't all bad.

Then there were the movie premieres. Red carpets! Shiny, tacky limos! The disco sparkle of flashing cameras! Beautiful people in inappropriately revealing ensembles! Sadly, those spectacles were only a small part of the affair. For those of us manning our little production office off the Sunset Strip, the days before a big premiere were spent fielding calls from the 'entitled set,' those people who, while having had nothing at all to do with the making of the film in question, felt that by virtue of their elevated standing in Hollywood they deserved a ticket and a space in the coveted reserved sanctum in the middle of the theatre, where plush seats were cordoned off for the movie's stars, director, and producer. And my comrades and I – Bryan, our wisecracking and kind office manager; Lillian, our thoughtful and lovely VP of development; Maggie, our svelte and multitasking VP of physical production; and Dori, the mistress of all things that needed to be done in Sandy's personal and business life – the five of us spent those days leading up to the premiere explaining to the arrogant shits on the other end of the line that Sandy had the audacity to give away all her reserved tickets to crew members who actually worked their asses off on the film and never got invited to these kinds of events. By the time I walked up the red carpet, I was cranky and not at all in the mood for flashing lights, pretty people, and small talk.

It was during this time that my mother got sick. Colon cancer. Colon cancer after she lived her life doing everything right. She ate organic and ran marathons. She never dyed her hair; it was still shiny nutmeg brown. She had no wrinkles and she could beat me cold in a push-up contest. In a few short years she was gone, and it got me wondering – what was the point again?

During those sad days after she died, I turned to the universal standby for combating melancholy. Sugar. Preferably sugar combined with majestically high volumes of butterfat and chocolate. Despite LA's bounty of type-2 diabetes-inducing snack havens, the Krispy Kremes and the glorious In-and-Out Burger, nothing I was shoving into my mouth was making me cheery. I cracked open my long-neglected cookbooks, weathered German baking tomes with recipes ripped from the *Washington Post* stuck in between the pages, loopy notes scribbled in the margins by my mother. I was craving something comforting and warm, something like an American cinnamon bun but without the full frontal sweetness. A mix between the elegant bittersweet chocolate my grandmother savoured in Germany, the doughy brightness of the jam-filled *krapfen* my mother bought at the corner bakery in her hometown of Nürnberg, and the chewy sweet yeast bomb peddled by the noxious Pillsbury Doughboy.

Back then in Hollywood, I was resentful of healthy living and becoming so emotionally guarded that I didn't trust the sincerity of anyone's motives, so I baked in search of balance and hope. And when I baked, the gentle sweetness and soft sponge of a well-made sticky bun soothed my growing bitterness at God and humanity. At the end of the day at work, I'd open a new document on my computer. Instead of detailed notes on the latest script, I'd lovingly list the ingredients

I needed from the grocery store. I'd choose a snappy font, writing each ingredient in **bold**, increasing the font size to distinguish this particular document as something apart from the other piles of paper on my desk. This piece of paper had my undivided attention.

All-Purpose Flour
Baker's Sugar
Granny Smith Apples (at least 8)
Butter
Yeast

I'd print the list and the recipe. I'd staple the two together and find that I was momentarily relaxed and optimistic.

The more I baked, the more I conjured the long-dormant goofy kid who lived, schemed, and debauched for sweets.

I baked for friends who wanted nothing from me but my company and my pastries. This made me happy and left me feeling like a productive human. Apple pie, scones, croissants, chocolate cake, fruit tarts. Gorgeous doughs that filled our kitchen with the tangy, living smell of yeast, Danish and sticky buns doubling in size in the heat of our little oven. I baked because it made me content and fulfilled and it brought happiness to others. And along the way I became a master baker.

At first, I was a closet baker. No one outside of my close-knit circle knew my dirty secret – that I spent quality time in the kitchen. In Hollywood, I'd have had more street cred if I'd revealed that I was a crack-addled anorexic leper. But a baker? What kind of weak-minded, carb-consuming, domestically minded loser bakes? I should have been networking, attending screenings and cocaine-soaked after-parties in my free time. My mom, if she had been around, she'd have told me to be loud and proud, to not care what everyone thought. Her one wish for her daughters was that we never conform: 'Don't be normal. *Bitte*.' And Ray, my other great comfort during the dark years, he needed me to open the doors and distribute the wares of the bakeshop that had once been our kitchen. We were running out of room.

I was so consumed with passion for the flour arts that I was starting to slip at work. At meetings, I'd bring up baking at the strangest moments.

Studio Executive: 'I'm not buying this whole 'meet cute' scenario we've got in the current draft of the script. It feels contrived. Not the least bit romantic.'

Me: 'You're right. It's like making an apple pie. You start adding things to make it fancy and 'new' and it just tastes like crap. Instead of keeping it simple, letting the humble apple take centre stage.'

Executive: 'What?'

Since it was no longer a well-guarded secret, I started to bring the endless bounty of my baking to high-powered, sleekly catered executive confabs. Instead of shelling out hundreds on Bordeaux for a hostess gift at a producer's holiday party, I baked little sugar cookies and painted them with icing in loving detail. I brought pies to movie sets and carrot cakes for birthdays at the major studios. And I started to get requests. One director hadn't had a homemade strawberry-rhubarb pie since he was a kid. A writer wanted a decent corn muffin; he just couldn't find one outside of New York City.

In the midst of my pastry revolution, I woke one night to find I couldn't move and couldn't speak. I experienced a bout of partial sleep paralysis, but I think the colloquial term for it, 'a witching riding your back,' describes the experience more accurately. Despite my inability to use my voice, I had no trouble hearing. And something was indeed speaking to me; chanting was more like it. It was some of the most obnoxious woo-woo, airy-fairy drivel.

'Goodness and kindness, together as one. Goodness and kindness, together as one. Goodness and kindness, together as one.'

It just wouldn't stop. And since I was awake but paralysed, I had to listen to this nonsense bombarding my brain; it was a new age 2 a.m. car alarm. I have weird things like this happen once in a while. But it's usually when my arm's fallen asleep, and I'll wake Ray in a panic. 'Ray, I can't find my arm! I've lost my arm!' And he'll massage my dead arm into tingling pain.

I'll be perfectly honest; I understood the message, whether it was self-generated or celestial programming. I'd been forever struggling with my crossed wiring since childhood. On the one hand, I was born pathologically shy with severe misanthropic tendencies. From day one, I wanted nothing to do with humanity. To explain my antisocial rudeness, my family apologised by constantly repeating, 'That's Gesine, she's shy. Very, *very* shy.'

But along with my general distaste for bipeds, I battled with an overwhelming need to live well, to live righteously. I'd ask my mother, 'When will I grow out of this? When will I mature?' I thought that when you got to a certain age you would experience a biologically induced state of enlightenment, where all petty insecurities and distastes would disappear and you'd live a life of generosity and kindness.

But she told me, quite sadly, 'Sina, most people never mature.'

And boy, was she right. There I was in Los Angeles, a place dedicated to the pursuit of economic happiness and grotesque exposure. Where it's de rigueur to drop $2,000 on a prestige handbag that's meant to be utilised for a month and then forgotten in a growing pile of once-chic leather sacks. And the cycle begins again. More money, more animals sacrificed for a four-week spin on the bony arm of a fame-hungry bore. I wasn't witnessing any cathartic bouts of maturity. I was living at the epicentre of an ugly cesspool of mass consumption. And I was a part of it, because although I complained about it and found it repulsive, I wasn't changing it. To quote a rare human who evolved into a mature being, Ghandi would have told me, 'Be the change you want to see in the world.'

I didn't want more stuff. I wanted to be *more happy*. I wanted to be good. I wanted to stop hating people and start understanding. And the only way I knew how to feel like a good and kind person was through baking.

It took a long while to truly wake up and realise that the job and the life I'd been looking for, the one that was fulfilling and that fed my sugar-laced soul, was pastry. Everyone else knew it before I did.

Years later, completely out of the closet and living in Vermont as a professional baker, I returned to LA for Christmas. My friend Jonathon took me to a boutique on Rodeo Drive. His offices were around the corner and he popped in regularly to chat up the lovelies. I'd been there before when I still worked in Hollywood. The beautiful shopgirls weren't very nice the first time, and their replacements were exactly the bony prestige-handbag creatures I'd loathed when I lived there. But I had a gift certificate and I was determined to leave with something Vermont appropriate. They chatted with my charming friend and ignored me when they weren't giving me the stink eye. I approached the counter, $200 T-shirt in hand, and passed my gift certificate to the six-foot forty-pound blonde at the register. You'd have thought I'd given her a flaming bag of dog poo. And then Jonathon felt the need to make introductions.

'Girls, this is my friend Gesine. She's the one who makes the macaroons I brought you for Christmas.'

Their faces went slack. Uh-oh. What was he thinking, bringing these stick figures food? And then the blonde grinned, a smile so genuine I could see the tow-headed, Play Doh-eating rascal she must have been in kindergarten. As it turns out, they were all very pleased to meet me. And I was pleased to meet their funny and lovely alter egos too. That's why I bake. Sure, it makes *me* happy. But through baking, I get to be a modern incarnation of Saint Nikolaus, who releases the lovely children hiding in every guarded adult.

Back in the wee hours in Vermont when I'm alone in my kitchen, I work full of anticipation. Every pastry has the potential of making someone perfectly happy, of momentarily stripping them of adult worries and baggage. So while the world sleeps, I brew my coffee and wake myself to the reality of my one-woman pastry revolution. With a little caffeine magic ripping through my veins, I'm conjuring, not baking, creating pastry spells for your every ailment. So don't be offended if I still can't offer you a hug or even a smile as a gesture of warmth, but please take this little pastry. It embodies my goodness and kindness, together as one tasty treat.

Espresso Cheesecake

DURING THE SECOND WORLD WAR, Omi took her young family – my mother and her two sisters, my Tante Christel and Tante Erika – from bomb-ravaged Nürnberg to the safety of the Austrian Alps. And while the countryside was abundant in greenery and nature, coffee and other luxury items were hard to come by. When she could get her hands on them, she used every last bit of her cherished coffee beans, even adding the used grounds to the batter of small cakes so that nothing was wasted.

In the shop, we dump all of our used grounds into large tubs that local farmers pick up from the side of the bakery and add to their compost. But at the espresso station, there are small heaps of freshly ground beans that get cast by the wayside, excess black powder that's brushed from the portafilter basket before the espresso is firmly tamped into a neat coffee puck.

I gather these bits in a small plastic container and save them for espresso cheesecake, much like my Omi did with her precious soggy grounds, loathe to see all the flavourful goodness dumped into the trash. The base recipe for the cheesecake is my mother's. A feat of reverse engineering that would make Microsoft proud, my mother spent weeks dissecting the components of a particularly famous New York cheesecake until she had reproduced the thing perfectly in her own kitchen. Every cheesecake I make uses this base; it's a dense and serious thing. Not for the faint of heart or lactose intolerant. And laced with espresso, it's got a surprising kick for such a heavy and creamy cake.

MAKES ONE LARGE 8-INCH CHEESECAKE OR EIGHT MINI-SPRINGFORM CHEESECAKES

For the cookie crust
2 cups chocolate wafer cookies or Oreos, processed until very fine
½ pound (2 sticks) unsalted butter, melted

For the cheese filling
1¼ pounds cream cheese, softened
¾ cup sugar
¼ cup fresh espresso grounds – don't use soggy, used grounds. Grind fresh beans into a fine powder and add this directly to the batter.
3 large eggs plus 1 egg yolk
1 cup brewed coffee

1 tablespoon instant espresso added to the coffee

½ teaspoon vanilla extract

1½ tablespoons all-purpose flour

Baker's Note: If you've bought pre-ground espresso, regrind it in a small portable grinder. You want ultrafine bits of espresso – so fine that they appear almost like vanilla bean flecks. You don't want them to add crunch, just flavour.

FOR THE CRUST

Preheat the oven to 350°F/180°C.

Place the cookies in a small bowl, drizzle the butter over them, and stir, making sure the crumbs are evenly coated with butter.

Place the cookie crumbs in an ungreased 9-inch springform pan. With your hands, pat and spread the crumbs evenly over the bottom and about 2 inches up the sides of the pan. Bake in the centre of the oven for 5 minutes. Remove and set aside to cool to room temperature.

Lower the oven temperature to 200°F/95°C.

FOR THE FILLING

Place the cream cheese and sugar in the bowl of an electric mixer and, with the whisk attachment, beat on high until smooth. Add the espresso grounds and mix until incorporated.

Add the eggs one at a time, beating until each is completely incorporated. Add the egg yolk.

Add the coffee mixture, vanilla, and flour. Mix until smooth and all ingredients are well incorporated.

Pour the filling into the cooled crust and bake in the centre of the oven for a few hours – at least two hours, and maybe as long as four hours. You can check for doneness by giving the pan a little shake. If it wobbles like it's still very liquid in the centre, keep going. This could take hours. But I'm betting you want a cheesecake with a creamy-smooth consistency and no cracks. So just wait. If you give the cheesecake a shimmy and it jiggles just a little in the middle but otherwise seems nice and firm, turn off the oven but leave the cheesecake inside to cool slowly. Then remove the cheesecake from the oven and set aside to cool completely in the pan.

Unmould the cheesecake and refrigerate, uncovered, for at least 3 hours before serving.

Chapter Three

My Kingdom for a Scone

5 a.m.

THIS MORNING, in my beaten-up industrial Vermont kitchen, I stretch on tippy toes to reach for the power button of the radio that teeters on top of our towering double-doored fridge, and raucous music joins the low drone of the ovens. I unlock the side door for Tim, my right-hand man in the kitchen; he comes in just at 5 a.m. I have a solid block of time, about an hour, to spread my work over every flat space in the kitchen before he's due. I make choux paste in a ten-gallon stockpot for éclairs on one burner of the stovetop and on another set a small saucier of cream to boil for pastry cream. On a back burner, a water bath simmers under a metal bowl of chocolate and butter slowly melting into each other. Sometimes I manage to fit a small saucepan with fresh eggs from our store's den mother and number one pastry saleswoman, Bonnie – breakfast if I can remember to eat. I swing open the door of the little oven in the back and grab two trays filled with small cheesecakes that have been left setting overnight.

I get all the mixers spinning on the metal countertops, their high whine joining the chorus of the ovens and music. In the middle of this mechanised chorus, I start grinding pistachios for meringue and set the whole kitchen ablast with a percussive storm. If I've forgotten to unlock the side door for Tim, his banging won't break through my wall of sound.

A small splinter of light starts to break through the side window by the sinks. Tim arrives and we share the small kitchen space. Tim's built like a boulder, a head shorter than I and strong as an ox. He's been an instructor at the local culinary school, run a successful catering operation in D.C., and acted as a sous chef in renowned kitchens all across the States for decades, but he has ended up working with me as a baker in the middle of nowhere due to a set of convoluted circumstances possible only in the pastoral vortex that is Vermont.

We manoeuvre silently around each other in the hours before the store opens; I scoot out of the way when he needs flour or sugar from the bins under my workstation. He sidesteps when I need a pastry bag or parchment paper, small, barely audible grunts signalling that we just need to grab a little something. I've baked the éclair shells in the top oven and the pistachio meringue has just come out of the bottom, the cue that it's time for Tim to bump up the temperature, start brushing the delicate tops of the croissants with egg wash, and bake them.

Some pastries, like croissants, Danish, and sticky buns, require advance prep. We set aside blocks of time in the week to make a few days' worth of each. Croissant dough is an all-day affair, often stretching into two days. Separate elements, a three-pound butter block and the sticky dough, are rolled together, folded like a book, and then allowed to rest. Then rolled out again and folded just so. And then set to rest again. You repeat this a few more times and then refrigerate the tight bundle for hours, or overnight, until it is ready to be rolled out once again and cut into pert triangles for plain and raspberry croissants or into buttery rectangles for chocolate and savoury. I do this all by hand, forgoing modern space-hogging machinery that promises to take me out of the equation and poke, prod, and roll my dough into perfect proportions. Why let the machine have all the fun? Touching beautifully made dough, feeling the slight shift in texture from soggy to elastic as you knead, getting a bicep workout from shaping the dough by hand with my weathered French rolling pin, screwing up the measurements just a little so some triangles are longer and some fatter – there are emotional benefits that accumulate the more contact you have with a dough. The hours and days consumed by a single batch of croissant dough, assuming I haven't made a grievous mistake somewhere along the line, are sublime.

Then there's batter on the fly, things we make and bake as we need them: teacakes, Golden Eggs, chocolate hearts, chocolate cakes, and carrot cakes. All the ingredients go in one mixing bowl – add and mix the elements in the right order for the right amount of time, and you're ready to bake in minutes. And quick breads, like scones and biscuits, are things I've always made by hand – flour, leavening, salt, and sugar in a huge bowl. Add a few pounds of butter, cut into small pieces, and massage the butter into the flour with your fingers until it resembles a coarse meal. Add eggs and other wet ingredients and you've got scones. No fancy equipment, just your hands and good judgment. Of all the things we bake, it's the smell of a hot savoury scone that stops me in my tracks and entraps me. Knowing that we can mix up a batch in minutes if we've been wiped out in front or if I've got a craving is a beautiful thing.

Once the quick stuff is mixed and baking, we roll

out puff pastry shells for fruit tarts and cream tarts. At some point, we agreed on a system without ever talking about it. What we do and when we do it in the twilight hours of the early morning evolved naturally. I never scheduled a meeting to discuss it. We don't have a memo filed away outlining our morning baking protocol.

The morning bake isn't so much a routine as a meditation. I'm making the same things as yesterday but it's not monotonous. It's a chance to make things better, or to transform the same old into something new. I find myself thinking about the people I love. And how I've loved the same few people for most of my life but, like baking the identical things every morning, those relationships never get boring. Often I think about my dad.

I was a mama's girl; Mom had my undivided devotion. So during her lifetime, my father and I were never close.

Except when it came to food. Talking about food, especially anticipating a future meal, was the height of vulgarity for my mother. But Dad and I could talk companionably for hours about dinner at breakfast and about breakfast at lunch. The circumstances in which we actually looked forward to eating were limited; my mother maintained strict dietary control at all times. We'd have to be on vacation and far, far away from an operational oven. So when the opportunity presented itself, we would nurse a meal by talking about if for days beforehand.

In the summer of 1982, when I was twelve, we dropped my sister off at college in North Carolina. And then Mom announced she'd landed a job at the Chattanooga Opera in Tennessee. She was leaving me alone with Dad for weeks.

I locked myself in my room and read. I was perfectly ready to go without food for a few weeks. I'd never seen Dad cook and didn't expect him to start, so there was a good likelihood that only Mom's leftovers were on deck. Reheating additive-free gruel spawns fiendish flavours and textures. I'd have none of it.

My plan was scrapped when one morning a wonderful smell pulled me out of Tolkien's Middle-earth.

I closed my book and waited. The aroma kept coming, small popping sounds announcing waves of deep-fried goodness seeping in under my door. I shuffled down the hall and poked my head into the kitchen. Dad was at the stove, effortlessly flipping a couple of paper-thin breaded steaks in a crackling frying pan. He moved with an economy of motion and grace that astounded me. I'd assumed he never cooked because he couldn't and wouldn't. But here he was. Making chicken-fried steak. He'd made eggs, too.

He was a relaxed cook but meticulous, cleaning

as he went, taking pains to organise the kitchen for optimum efficiency. And when he cooked, I asked him questions. About what he was making and where he learned. Slow-cooked hominy grits with a generous hunk of melting butter vibrating with the soul of the Deep South led to stories of Birmingham, penny candy, fluffy biscuits drenched in gravy, five-cent matinees with my aunts Luddy, Tippy, and Sis, and driving barefoot without a steering wheel through the neighbourhood. We were uncharacteristically comfortable with each other those few weeks, bonded by my mother's absence and a love of forbidden foods.

We slipped back into our workaday silence when Mom returned. But we'd discovered a way to communicate, and once in a while we'd find ourselves chatting companionably over our mutual admiration for ultra-high-butterfat ice cream or Star Trek or cars, and we'd enjoy each other's company.

In the quiet hours before we open, I think about my father. As I mix butter, flour, and sugar, I'm relaxed and accepting. I can see all those parts of my mother, my father, my grandmother, and my sister, all mixed up to make me. Since we've both lost the woman we loved and since I've become a baker, we're closer. We're made of some of the same ingredients, some that are unappealing but others that we admire. And we'll always share an appreciation for good food, like biscuits with gravy and sweet scones.

Cream Scones

SCONES AND BISCUITS are by far the easiest break-fast pastries to master. You don't need any heavy equipment, there's no tricky yeast involved, and you can fudge with the innards. They're also delicious and heartwarming. Scones are something of a biscuit but with more subtlety and charm. They have a crumbly, slightly sweet allure that invites compulsive eating.

MAKES 8 SCONES

½ cup heavy cream, plus additional for
    brushing the scones
1 large egg
1 teaspoon lemon extract
3 tablespoons sugar, plus additional for
    sprinkling the scones
2¼ cups all-purpose flour
½ teaspoon salt
1 tablespoon baking powder
6 tablespoons (¾ stick) cold unsalted butter, cut
    into bits
½ cup dried cranberries

Preheat the oven to 400°F/200°C.

In a bowl whisk together the cream, egg, lemon, and sugar until well combined.

In another bowl stir together the flour, salt, and baking powder; blend in the butter with your fingers until the mixture resembles coarse meal.

Stir in the cranberries and the cream mixture with a fork until the mixture just forms a sticky but manageable dough.

Knead the dough gently on a lightly floured surface for 30 seconds, pat it into a ½-inch-thick circle, and cut out rounds with a 1½-inch fluted cutter.

Gather the scraps, repat the dough, and cut out more rounds. Place the scones on an ungreased baking sheet. Brush with cream and sprinkle with sugar.

Bake the scones in the middle of the oven for 15 to 18 minutes, or until golden.

Savoury Rock Scones

TIM CREATED THESE addictive morsels by jerry-rigging an already fabulous sweet Rock Scone recipe to accommodate savoury ingredients. The glorious scent of these pastries baking is almost as wonderful as their taste.

MAKES 12 SCONES

5 cups all-purpose flour

¾ pound (3 sticks) unsalted butter

¼ cup sugar

½ teaspoon cayenne

1 teaspoon salt

1½ tablespoons baking powder

1½ cups nonfat buttermilk

1 large egg

1 cup cubed tasso ham (or sautéed lardons)

½ cup grated Gruyère cheese

Preheat the oven to 350°F/180°C.

Work the flour, butter, sugar, cayenne, salt, and baking powder with your fingers until the mixture resembles cornmeal and all of the butter is well incorporated.

Add the buttermilk, egg, tasso, and Gruyère and continue to work the mixture gently with your hands until the dough is uniformly wet and no dry clumps of flour remain. Be careful not to overwork the dough.

Scoop fistfuls of dough and mound them on an ungreased baking sheet, spacing them a few inches apart. Bake until brown and cooked through, about 25 minutes.

Chapter Four

Be Nice to Your Mother (Sponge)

6 a.m.

A S I MIX AND ROLL, periodically stopping by the
coffeepot to top off my never-ending cup of joe,
I look out the window at the street and Terry's parking
lot just beyond. As it gets lighter, Terry's SUV turns in
next to the Dumpsters we share and he carries in the
local papers the deliveryman dumped at his front door.
Seconds later our morning barista, Lily, drags herself
in to open up the espresso and coffee stations, hair wet
from the shower and eyes still puffy with sleep.

Lily starts layering sounds onto our kitchen beat.
The coffee grinder roars for minutes at a time, the
espresso machine hissing and humming as she pulls

shots, adjusting the espresso grind by tiny increments to compensate for any atmospheric conditions that can make it bitter or sour. The purr of the steam wand creates whirlpools of dense foam in milk as she makes me a morning cappuccino, adding another layer of caffeination to my buzzing system. Ray comes in through the front door a half hour before opening, whistling. The light is coming in bright waves and Tim and I start racing to get everything from the kitchen to the pastry case.

Tim finishes the éclairs, slicing the crispy choux pastry in half and filling the bottom with fluffy sweet pastry cream. He drenches the top with chocolate glaze and rests each one in a gold-rimmed paper boat fashioned specifically to keep a wobbly éclair stable. Lemon tarts, baked at 5:30 a.m. and now cool, are ready for an austere ring of meringue and then a touch from the torch to brown them. I've unmoulded the chocolate mousse cakes from their stainless steel rings by gently warming the metal with a heat gun. These four-inch cylindrical towers of deep dark decadence, sitting atop a round sliver of dense flourless chocolate cake, are so high they have to be placed on the very top shelf of the display case or they'll get decapitated. The raspberry mousse tarts are shockingly pink, but formed into little hearts they are coy beauties, shining demurely with a sweet glaze brushed on top. Sometimes, if I'm feeling fancy, I'll pipe a chocolate rose at the top and then a slender stalk that reaches to the pointy tip of the heart, adding petite chocolate thorns along the way.

I make last touches on cakes for the cold case and Tim shuttles from the kitchen to the front, balancing silver platters carefully piled with crispy croissants, turnovers, scones, and sticky buns. I'm right behind with long metal trays lined with parchment paper and arranged with pastries that find a home inside the refrigerated case. Bonnie's exuberant entrance marks the countdown, fifteen minutes to open. She sets the front of the shop to rights, wiping down the marble tables and filling up the sugar bowls and creamers. She cranks up Abba's 'Dancing Queen' and opens the doors for the waiting regulars.

When we opened our doors on August 3rd, 2004, we'd taken months of our lives and all of our savings to transform our tiny shop into a pastry haven. We painted the original wood siding of our turn-of-the-last-century shotgun general store a muted putty, busted out the dingy plate glass, enlarged the windows in the front, and hired a local artisan to painstakingly apply gold leaf lettering by hand to read 'Gesine Confectionary' on one window and 'Gesine Gourmet' on the other.

We gutted everything to the studs and rebuilt the innards, painting the new Sheetrocked walls a grey blue, the hundred-year-old tin ceiling an oyster-shell white, and the wood shelving a lacquered black, every paint chosen from original paint samples from colonial New England. We refinished the floors, brought in a new pastry case, and put in an oak counter. We installed muted lighting and hung framed black-and-white photos from family childhood birthday parties. There's one of Ray's mom in elementary school, holding up a cake and grinning like she's going to eat the entire thing. There's me at five in a checkered party dress with my arms flung around two empty dining room chairs, a paper crown sitting on my pigtailed head. I'm looking grumpy. The table is decked out with plates and a beautiful dark chocolate cake with jazzy white piping on the sides. If it had a caption, it would read, 'Let's get this party started already. I want cake.'

We bought small bar-height marble tables and brought our own hand-turned Windsor chairs from home and placed them up front. On the right wall next to the large wine cooler sits an imposing sixteenth-century Spanish church pew that my sister had shipped up from an antiques shop in Savannah, Georgia, for my birthday. Owls are carved on either side underneath the armrests. On the top of the tall black display shelves that line the walls, Ray has started a gallery of oddities. The vast majority of our collection is composed of owl tchotchkes our customers find when they're cleaning out their attics, along with other items that find their way into the shop: a Mexican wrestling mask, a bottle of Donald Trump cologne, and a yellow bucket that says, 'Don't release the bird.'

It's all elegant and a bit austere. But it's also quaint,

inviting, and a little strange. A lot like the rest of Montpelier.

In the back, in the bakery, the floor is linoleum, the work surfaces are metal, the equipment is industrial, and the lighting is fluorescent and terribly unflattering. We have a cramped office at the very back with a desk, a computer, and an ever-rotating heap of inventory that we really need but can't quite figure out how to organise: packing supplies, labels for our candies, extra boxes for boxed lunches, stray cookbooks. Mainly, we just have to keep it simple, because it's in the back that it can get crazy, with flour flying everywhere and two bakers in sensible shoes running around with their heads cut off. But it's also where the beautiful things we make require space in which to be created. And despite the fact that we built all of this to provide a space for the genesis of sweet pastries, at 6 a.m. it's bread that gets all the attention.

Every day, we produce forty-eight small loaves, both white and wheat. Even though we're primarily a pastry joint catering to interstitial munchies and not the square meal, like most bakeries, we need to bring in business at all hours. So we started to do lunch, crispy panini, to keep those midday hours profitable. But this also gives us an excuse to make bread every day.

Contemplate your average grocery store loaf of bread. The wheat is most likely genetically modified and doused with a payload of pesticides. Then it's processed, stripped of nutrients, and pulverised into oblivion. It's mixed with preservatives to allow for an abnormally long shelf life. And then it's cut into slices of fascist uniformity.

But the great tragedy of today's bread isn't so much the radioactive sludge from which it is made. The tragedy is that we've lost the sense of community behind bread.

There was a time when bread was made in a communal oven; when families, using their own particular recipe, would mix, shape, and proof their bread at home and then walk the few miles along country roads, meeting neighbouring families along the way on the same journey, and bake their bread in a town oven. Families carved their initials or a family symbol into the dough to tell theirs apart and the many families kibitzed as the oven did its work. Then they walked the long miles back, warm crusty loaves along for the ride, to make dinner and break bread together.

I'm not one to judge. My all-time favourite food is grilled cheese. And I only make it with not-found-in-nature orange processed cheese and white bread. The kind of bread you can smush into a tight ball, put in your pocket, and save to use at the driving range. I'll make a few sandwiches and eat them all alone, full of guilt. I berate myself for falling so low: that bread, that cheese, that pound of butter I used to fry those nasty bits into crispy, melted perfection. Then I set the bread aside and let it get mouldy.

But when we make a loaf of bread in our little kitchen,

we use beautiful flour and the simplest ingredients. We dote over the starter, our homegrown yeast, and the rising dough, carefully fashioning smooth rounds and waiting patiently until the bread is ready for the oven. And we'll talk about it, wondering whether we forgot the salt, pondering the possibility of selling the whole loaves to our customers instead of using it all for sandwiches.

There's no chance I'll easily forget that it's around, or subject it to the indignity of processed cheese food. As a matter of fact, I'll take pictures of the especially handsome rounds, and sometimes I feel like wrapping a loaf in a bow and taking it on a grand tour of the neighbourhood for everyone to see; I'm so proud of it. I want everyone to share in the miracle. My feelings are terribly hurt if I see someone throwing away even a corner of crust from our bread.

Mom made her own bread. It wasn't half bad when it came right out of the oven. It was when the loaf cooled and we actually put it to a purpose that it became a disaster. It had all the qualities of pumice with none of the structure. It fell to pieces the second you started slicing it. At the school cafeteria, surrounded by grossed-out kids, I would reveal the horror that was the crumbly macrobiotic sandwich: tofu bologna, tofu simulated cream cheese, and walnuts. Huge crumbs of whole-grain bread, studded with small walnuts held on by a filmy layer of cream cheese on top of a limp slice of faux soy bologna. And it all lay in a crumbly blob at the bottom of the plastic bag.

I usually tossed my lunch and used my milk money to buy cookies. I did this with regularity and nonchalance. This false security came to bite me in the ass when my mother just happened to stop by during lunch and caught me mid-dunk at the trash bin.

'What did you throw away?' she asked with her German accent coming on mean and strong.

'Uh, just trash.' I'm a horrible liar.

'Take it out.'

I had to dig deep; the weight of seven whole grains can really cut a swath through Twinkie wrappers. She made me lay out the contents in front of the whole of Woodmont Elementary. They'd seen the horror of my lunches before but only as a parlour trick. A sight gag, if you will. They'd never seen anything from the brown bag consumed.

'Eat it.'

Where to start? Do I eat the crumbs on the bottom first or do I nibble at the exposed perimeter of limp faux meat product, gathering courage as I approach the core? My schoolmates were losing their appetites, packing up spongy white breaded ham sandwiches layered with neon mustard, leaving their chewy fruit roll-ups by the wayside as they trickled past me and headed outside for recess. You could see a few kids battling with internal conflict, they wanted to enjoy the show but couldn't risk Mrs. Bullock turning on them and demanding they partake as well.

I got through it, gag reflex working overtime, and never approached the lunchroom Dumpster with confidence again.

But now that I make my own bread, I understand my mother. The loaves I make aren't as packed with whole grains and dense nutritional fortitude. They're the lighter, fluffier version. But she made a starter, as I do. She tended to the dough as it was rising. She kneaded with her bare hands, and when the bread was finished baking, she'd always cut it while it was still warm and give us a beautiful steaming slice adorned with a smear of fresh butter. We'd sit at the table, the whole family, and admire the miracle of fresh bread. So what if it lost some it its lustre when it cooled; if I'd looked in everyone's lunch box that day, I'd have been the only kid who was lucky enough to have a mom who baked her kid bread. So to see me carelessly throw away the thing she'd made with so much love – that must have really hurt her. At the very least, it really pissed her off.

I'm constantly surrounded by all manner of sweets now, making anything that I'd ever dreamt of as a kid. And I make exactly the kind of bread that I want to tear into and share with my friends and neighbours. But I'd do anything for a loaf of bread made with loving nutritional kindness by my mother. She wouldn't believe me for a second, but I'd choose her crumbly, whole-grain-peppered bread over anything else.

Focaccia

FOCACCIA DOUGH is a multipurpose Italian beauty and very simple to master. I use it to make bouncy round loaves for sandwiches. But the same stuff can be stretched and flattened to make traditionally shaped focaccia – dimpled, flat, and sprinkled with rosemary, garlic, and onion. Or roll it flatter and round for a perfect pizza dough. You can measure the dough into small balls for dinner rolls or shape it into a hearty loaf. There are infinite delicious uses and very little work involved.

Of course, the process could entrance you and lead you down the devotional path of the artisan. But you can't say I didn't warn you.

MAKES ONE LARGE FOCACCIA

One ¼-ounce package active dry yeast (2½ teaspoons)

5 cups all-purpose flour, plus additional for kneading

¼ cup plus 3 tablespoons extra virgin olive oil, plus additional for the bowl and pan

2½ teaspoons table salt

1 tablespoon finely chopped fresh rosemary
1 teaspoon coarse sea salt

Stir together 1⅔ cups lukewarm (105° to 115°F or 40° to 45°C) water and the yeast in the bowl of an electric mixer and let stand until foamy, about 5 minutes.

Add the flour, ¼ cup of the oil, and table salt and beat with the paddle attachment at medium speed until a dough forms. Replace the paddle with the dough hook and knead at low speed until the dough is soft, smooth, and sticky, 3 to 4 minutes.

Lightly oil a large bowl. Turn the dough out onto a lightly floured surface and knead in 1 to 2 tablespoons more flour. Knead the dough 1 more minute (it will still be slightly sticky), then transfer to the bowl and turn the dough to coat it with oil. Let rise, covered with plastic wrap, at warm room temperature (about 70°F/20°C) until doubled in bulk, 1 to 1½ hours.

Generously oil a 15 x 10-inch baking pan. Press the dough evenly into the pan and cover it completely with a damp kitchen towel. Let the dough rise in a warm corner of the room until doubled in bulk, about 1 hour.

While the dough is rising, preheat the oven to 425°F/220°C.

Stir together the rosemary and remaining 3 tablespoons oil. Make shallow indentations all over the dough with your fingertips, then brush with the rosemary oil, letting it pool in the indentations. Sprinkle sea salt evenly over the focaccia and bake in the middle of the oven until golden, 20 to 25 minutes.

Immediately set a rack over the pan and flip the focaccia onto it, then turn right side up. Serve warm or at room temperature.

Chapter Five

Montpeculiar

6:45 a.m.

'WE'RE GOING TO NEED MORE SOY.' Lily pokes her head into the kitchen and gives me the bad news.

'By saying that, do you mean we'll need soy in the foreseeable future or that you just went to make a drink and realised that we have no soy at all?'

'We have no soy at all.'

In a few short hours, Tim and I have filled our little shop with hundreds of pastries. We don't stop to congratulate ourselves. We have to keep moving, prepping, baking, rolling until we close so we can do this all over again tomorrow morning. And I have to run a ridiculous last-minute errand into town to get soy. We have ten people on staff: Tim and I are in the kitchen, we have a rotating carnival of dishwashers, and at least two counter people are in the front at all times. Ray, when he's in town, is the consummate jack-of-all-trades, making the best cappuccinos and chatting up the customers like an old pro. He maintains and fixes all of our heavy equipment and designs labels for the new products we keep churning out of the back. When he's gone, working in Hollywood, there's a huge void, not only in my home life but in our store. It also means that I'm on deck as errand boy.

Ah, the glamour of small-business ownership. It's filled with so much more than fifteen hours of baking. There's soymilk. Or the lack of it. Or we've run out of a certain size of pastry box or the butter wasn't delivered or the propane has run out and the ovens aren't heating. Of all places, the crunchiest and most hippified state in our union, and I can't get a soy milk vendor to deliver. So just before we open our doors at 7 a.m., I have to journey to our local grocer, a rundown, vinyl-encased mecca to limp produce and jug wine. Strangely, they carry the only organic soy that makes decent lattes, so I'm stuck making this trip a few times a week, shedding layers of flour with each step I take down the dairy aisle.

I should be grateful, because this is the only time I get a peek at the outside world. I tear off my flour-coated apron and pull on my tatty black puffer jacket. My pants have taken on what the apron didn't cover, so the bottom ten inches of my pants down to my shoes have a layer of white while everything else is relatively flour free. There might be some on my face. Big deal. I wash my hands quickly; it takes too long to get every bit of dough out of my nails so I settle for looking slightly ghoulish.

I pile into my mud-encrusted Subaru and swing out onto Elm Street toward downtown, past the latter-day hippies living in colourful, patchouli-scented communal disarray in ramshackle colonial mansions dotting our neighbourhood. As I get closer to State and Main, I pass Pam's soup shop, That's Life Soup. Pam used to be a regular. She'd come in daily, wrapped in her feather-stuffed puffer jacket, her knee-high black rubber muck boots paired with a diaphanous skirt, her grey-streaked hair hastily snatched up in a tie and stray pieces dancing around her rosy cheeks. She'd get a mocha and stay for a spell. Then she started to deliver stockpots full of soup, worried that we weren't catching a break to eat – Shaker Chicken Soup, creamy and soulful; spicy Vietnamese Pho, a steamy firecracker broth tamed by pliant rice noodles. Soup to Pam is like pastry to me. She is consumed by a passion for all things broth, and her devotion is rewarded with beautifully rendered savoury elixirs. Bolstered by our success and her own talent, she opened a shop down the road and we've barely seen her since. Occasionally we'll run into each other in the wee hours of the morning in the produce aisle, rummaging for decent last-minute ingredients.

Artie's Thai restaurant, the Royal Orchid, is just across from Pam's. Artie adds some much-needed international glamour to our quaint street. He runs something of an exchange program, flying his countrymen and women from Thailand for stints at his place, conveniently leaving out descriptions of our six-month snowbound winter and talking up the American dream. And we benefit from their otherworldly skills in the kitchen. But despite our shared oppressive workload, we all seem to find time to pop in to each other's establishments to complain about taxes and lack of sleep.

I slow down at the hippie café, minding the patchy-bearded string beans propping themselves against the bricks. There's no telling when they'll rouse themselves from their weed coma and dart into oncoming traffic in search of a drum circle. I make sure to avoid eye contact with 'mean Santa,' an appealingly white-bearded gentleman dressed in folksy garb who stops unexpectedly midstride to lustily rant about the sin and evil breathing inside every woman. Come spring, I keep my eyes peeled for the naked guys. Now and again some local young folk saunter down the streets in their birthday finest in celebration of spring's awakening, taking full-frontal advantage of our liberal laws regarding public nudity. (State law allows for public nudity, just not in state parks. Window-shopping au naturel is fine, but the law stipulates that you may not draw undue attention to your genitalia while doing so.)

Ray and I moved here unaware of the deeply ingrained oddness of the place and with some otherwise very misguided expectations. Mainly we imagined having a relaxing, simpler life, one where we didn't have to work all the time.

Initially, we hadn't intended to move permanently at all. Before I was terminally unhappy in LA, we toyed with the idea of getting a Northeast vacation refuge, a small cottage in a precious town brimming with quirky townsfolk. We'd pop in for short visits to Woodstock and Stowe, maintaining the charmed distance of summer folk. Staying just long enough to get to know the citizens on a first-name basis and take in a few anecdotes to bring back to civilisation, stories of woodsy eccentrics and quaint mom-and-pop shops.

But on an innocent getaway to Hanover, New Hampshire, to catch the homecoming football game at Ray's alma mater, Dartmouth, something peculiar happened when we took in the sights of neighbouring Vermont. Just as we crossed the state line from New Hampshire to Vermont, just as we drove over the upper Connecticut River on the Ledyard Bridge and headed into Norwich, Vermont, I subconsciously began to pull up stakes everywhere else and started planting them in the Green Mountains. Every spring, since I was a kid, the women of our household sniffed the air, trying to catch a fleeting scent that carried reminders and memories of Germany. The air was infused with that fresh scent in Vermont; I didn't have to chase after it.

Each town welcomed us with a whitewashed church spire, waving from above the treetops, and opened into a town square complete with a comely town hall and a turn-of-the-century general store with a pump-before-you-pay gas station circa 1950. There were no billboards needling us from the roadside to come and visit the industrial grease shack that was just 5 miles, 1 mile, 500 yards, 100 yards THIS EXIT!!! Small towns kindly introduced themselves and then courteously disappeared from view as we drove along the thick pine-lined roads. I'd found home.

We chose Montpelier, Vermont. We packed up everything we owned and shipped it across the country. There was a culinary school in town; for once I wanted to go to school because I was passionate about the subject, even if I'd be as old as the teachers. I was self-taught in every baking technique I knew of, but I figured I could always learn a trick or two at school.

When we first moved in 2004, we ventured far outside the ten-mile radius of what was to become our little shop. We were enjoying a very relaxing life in Vermont, just as we'd planned. We ate well and frequently, we slept in, and we spent hours curled up in leather chairs at the foot of our roaring wood-burning fireplace, reading and sketching. I even baked a bit and sent out care packages to family and friends with my latest sweet inventions. Mostly macaroons; they tended to be everyone's favourite. And Ray painted and sketched.

The macaroons I made – French almond macaroons to be exact – were the kind of treat that got everyone saying, 'Hey, you should go into business with these.' Why macaroons? Because they reminded me of my mom.

She adored marzipan and its cousin, the *mandelhoernchen*. *Mandelhoernchen* are the pastry equivalent of a baked pound of almond paste but with a few added textural components. A crisp outer skin, browned in the oven and covered with toasted sliced almonds but still dense, moist, and fragrantly almond inside. It's shaped into a horn, to mimic the majestic antlers of the alpine billy goat, the ends usually but not always dipped in dark chocolate.

I scoured the Internet and every one of my cookbooks for recipes. Among the millions of things that torment you when someone you love dies is not being able to ask them how they made something. Or where they hid a recipe. I couldn't find *mandelhoernchen* but I kept coming across *macaron*. The original macaroon, with almond. No coconut. Invented by Italian monks and later adopted by French nuns who baked the confections for pocket money while they were on the run during the French Revolution. It had the general ingredients of a *mandelhoernchen*, it was linked to divinity, and it had the power to save people from the guillotine. Who was I not to try it?

It was mighty tasty. I worked on the recipe until it was übertasty. It's not as showy as the shiny, chocolate-dipped horn; it's pretty much the Ethel Merman of pastry. Doesn't look like much, but damn it's good.

Sandy was a big fan of my humble and dainty macaroons. She was also getting restless with my quiet life. She had reluctantly agreed that my leaving the production company made sense, since I was spending most of my time talking about what I was going to bake next instead of coming up with ideas for the next great summer blockbuster. She also conceded that leaving LA, a town where legislation will one day be enacted to ban carbohydrates, was a wise thing as well. But she is a woman of constant motion and invention, and she viewed my relative dormancy as a waste of productivity. She called one day to in the early spring of 2004 to inform me that my sedentary life would soon end and my baking life would take on a trajectory that I couldn't control.

'Do you mind if I mention your macaroons in an interview I'm doing for *In Style*?'

That past Christmas, I had handmade my old company's holiday gift, mixing, scooping, and baking thousands of macaroons in my cramped Vermont kitchen. Laying out finished macaroons, row after endless row, on our maple dining room table. Packing a hundred tins, boxing everything up for shipping, and then watching the FedEx guy slog his way up our snowy driveway and up the granite stairs to our house. He had to make this trip again and again, balancing shipping boxes filled with almondy Christmas joy up and down snow-sodden stairs and then artfully executing a slow, controlled slide down the driveway. Damn, it felt good to have produced all of those wonderful treats and then watch them leave.

So why not mention them in a national magazine with a readership in the millions? Was I delusional? Ignorant and unprepared? Cocky and stupid enough to think I could do it? Absolutely. I had told everyone in LA that I was leaving to become a baker; it might be wise to actually start the transformation and get off my ass. But I hadn't yet focused on the specific direction my life as a baker would take. I could be a corporate megaproducer à la Mrs. Fields, or I could keep it small and diverse, à la the fantasy of *Chocolat*. If I was going to make a career out of this, I'd have to ponder these things.

There were differences of opinion regarding the name of our new business. I thought we should call it Helga's, after my mother. My friend, Marc, in a tip of his hat to my sick humour and lack of interpersonal skills, lobbied hard for me to call my shop 'Master

Baker! Eat It and Beat It!' But Ray thought we should name it Gesine, memorable if only because it was impossible to pronounce. It was a name no one else would have or want, except for me because it was, for better or worse, my own name. And that made it easy to trademark and effortless to secure the domain name on the Web.

The logo was easy. Along with being nicknamed Eule, my mother wore a gold owl amulet her whole life, and now I wear it as my own totem. Nothing would be more representative of what I was doing than my mother and her wise owl. Ray drew our mascot in a night.

But I couldn't bake out of our house. Health codes prohibit commercial baking enterprises from operating out of homes with animals. We had three. So we looked for a small place to do the baking. There aren't a lot of options when the store frontage is packed into ten blocks. There was an abandoned restaurant in the basement of an office building; it had been submerged in the flood of 1992. Every store in town has a picture of canoes paddling up the middle of State Street. I didn't want to invest thousands of dollars in an empty space just to have it suffer the fate of another flood. But Ray remembered something, a little shop tucked away from the town centre, sitting at the edge of a branch of the Winooski River in a neighbourhood called the Meadow. The single plate glass window of the ancient general store was covered with plywood. Once we'd chipped through the ice holding the front door fast, we entered a frozen den of rat poop, burst pipes, and rot. But we saw something in the eighteenth-century original tin ceiling and the small patch of weathered barn plank floors that had survived the years. And in the back, if we replaced the wood covering the cracked back windows, we'd have a view of the river. We could even clean out the back patch of lawn that had become the neighbourhood's tinsel-strewn Christmas tree graveyard and build a deck.

So we dug into our savings and bought the ugly little building at the edge of town. Then we tore out its insides until they were reduced to floor joists and dirt. We hired local carpenters, Skip and Bob, to rebuild her to her former understated glory, original tin ceiling and all.

While the little shop was under construction, we decided to utilise the services of the Vermont Food Venture Center, an organisation dedicated to helping small-time food entrepreneurs get off their feet by providing a facility to make their products and guidance in formulating them for a mass market. I was going to be a big-time entrepreneurial baker lady.

I packed up all of my gear and ingredients in neat rows in the back of my shiny new Subaru. I broke out my pressed chef's jacket and knife-pleated chef's pants, and took my new clogs out of the box for their first professional test drive; I'd bought them for school but macaroons sidetracked my pastry education. I pulled my hair back neatly yet attractively and applied just a touch of makeup. I was ready to drive to Fairfax, Vermont, a scenic cow-filled hour-long drive from Montpelier.

But unlike an LA commute, there was no time stopped in traffic. I spent the entire hour in motion, driving through beautiful farmland and suddenly dropping down into hills distorted by frost heaves, skidding through mud trenches on the back roads. My meticulously packed wares slid willy-nilly in the back of the car, mixers, scales, and a box of random tools mingling freely with my ski paraphernalia and a forgotten gardening spade.

The Venture Center is half of the town of Fairfax, the putty-coloured paint on its ancient wood siding peeling off in sheets. There's no address and very few windows, a door floating in the centre of the building and then a more inviting entrance off to the side, with a porch shielding it from the elements and a side driveway for delivery trucks.

I parked at the back and scrambled up the hill leading to the side door, my sparkly new baker's clogs slipping off my feet, the gluey mud sucking the wooden heels and holding them tight. I crab-walked the rest of the way. I bumped open the door with my hip, holding tight to my mud-spattered equipment, and met with a wall of stewed stench: bubbling tomatillos, hot peppers, onions, and tomatoes. My eyes teared up viciously, my tasteful mascara application sliding off my lashes and streaming down my cheeks. A tinny Grateful Dead number was just ending and the music segued seamlessly into an equally vile Phish tune. I caught sight of a hairnetted, tie-dyed young man, eyes fiery from prolonged exposure to stewing hot sauce or cannabis. I was guessing both.

'Hey! I'm here to see Bryan?'

'Dude, yeah, you're the cookie lady! He's just up the stairs. You have an accident on the way or something?'

I ran up the stairs as fast as I could to get away from the overwhelming stench of smouldering hot sauce. I pushed open the rickety hollow-core door and was relieved to find the room stink free and Bryan reassuringly middle-aged, khakied, and sober.

We went through my game plan, which was none. I only knew what I was making, how I made it, and that I'd have to know how to make lots of it, all at once, the minute the magazine hit the shelves.

'What's the shelf life of your product?'

'Um, I don't know. They usually get eaten right away.'

'What's the nutritional breakdown of the product, for your label?'

'Um, I don't have one.'

'How are you intending to package the product for safe delivery?'

'No clue.'

'What's your production schedule? How do you plan to store your ingredients, finished product, packaging materials? Are you registered to do business in the state of Vermont? And do you realise you'll have to wear a hairnet while baking here?'

Bryan gave me some tips, including the number of a woman who was a professional nutritionist and would breakdown my recipe for a government-approved label. He also gave me the number of a woman who'd had similar exposure in a magazine and had survived being slammed with an unforeseen number of orders.

Most days I was the only baker in the entire facility. I'd switch on the radio, start up the ovens, and begin making the dough. Every so often, there'd be a group making pies for a frozen apple pie company, hauling around barrels full of butter to the mixer and then pressing out rounds of dough, one by one, in a pie press, always weighing each piece of dough carefully and then subjecting the round blob to the blunt force trauma of a pie-plate-shaped weight that came slamming down and forced the stuff into shape. I never got sick of watching it. There were also the fudge ladies from Saratoga. They schlepped their equipment five hours across state lines to make vats of hot fudge. They bottled, labelled, and boxed for two to three days straight and when they were done, they'd be stocked with inventory for a couple of months. Midway through the process, punch drunk on cocoa fumes, they'd start tearing around the neighbouring kitchens and insisting that anything being made in the vicinity would benefit from a dunk in fudge. As the day wore down, the elder of the two fudge sisters, springy grey hair popping out from under her gauzy white hairnet, made a circuit around the compound. Stopping to chat with any young man who might be stuck working after hours, she'd invite him back to her Volvo for a beer, a smoke, and, of course, a free jar of hot fudge.

And then came the night that the magazine hit the stands. I sat in bed with my computer on my lap and hit the Refresh button every few minutes to see if I'd got any email orders. This kind of obsessive behaviour wasn't doing me any good, so I tried very hard to get invested in an earnest infomercial about adult acne products. But the beauty of the Internet allowed me to buy the product in minutes and get back to my maniacal clicking. No orders. Nothing. I was convinced that the buildup had been for nothing and I was sitting with a backload of product, packaging materials, and shipping boxes and, by now, a newly renovated storefront that would remain empty for generations to come. I slept fitfully, my scooping hand throbbing, our checkbook depleted, and my baking pride wounded.

When I woke, I immediately flipped open my laptop. My finger hovered over the Enter button. Then I tapped lightly, almost daring it not to respond. The screen popped up and my inbox had a few visitors. Almost a hundred. And they were mostly orders. Many were general inquiries, like 'would you get me an autographed picture of your sister' or 'can you get my script to your sister' or 'will you get your sister to go out with me.'

But mostly they were honest-to-goodness orders. And they kept coming each time I checked my inbox: ten new orders, twenty orders, one hundred orders. It was enough to give me a sense of accomplishment but not too many to be overwhelming. My communal workstation at the Food Venture Center became a genuine production line, golden macaroons gingerly packed in a shiny tin, heat-sealed, and nestled in a shipping box lined with a healthy wad of recycled packing material and festive tissue paper; a shiny owl sticker fastened the tissue before the box got sealed shut and affixed with a shipping label. 'Thank you for your order!' It was official. I was in business.

Today I have to remind myself, while I'm backing out of the driveway and heading downtown in a search for soy or running some other tedious errand, that I'm far more content baking fifteen hours a day and running mundane errands in New England than I ever was making movies in LA. I'm also far from maintaining any kind of 'summer folk' distance from Vermont. To the contrary, now I'm local colour; I'm the female version of the hot-sauce guy, with my lackadaisical sartorial style and my weathered car. I wave at the early-morning regulars, clutching their Gesine-branded travel mugs, as they push open the front door of the shop. The red door is wearing just at the place where everyone pushes it open and the front steps are grooved from traffic. These things were once shiny and new from our renovations just three years ago but are now, like us, marked by Vermont.

Starry Starry Nights

I CAN'T GIVE UP MY LIFEBLOOD, my macaroon recipe. Not for anything. How would I make a living? What would be special about them anymore, if the secrets in proportion and preparation escaped? Secrecy is a stingy peculiarity among bakers. Create a ballyhooed confection and you can be sure the recipe will be well guarded. And be particularly wary if, when prodded for the recipe, the baker gives it up. I can assure you that some key element has been purposely withheld. At a famous teahouse, my sister and I bought the cookbook that promised to reveal the culinary secrets of the establishment. Learning that a movie star was leaving with his tome, the resident baker hightailed it out of the kitchen with pen in hand. Instead of signing the cookbook, he flipped it open to the middle and made a small note in the margin of a particular page. 'I left out the salt and changed the ratio of butter,' he confessed sheepishly. True master bakers, surrounded by underlings watching every nuance, will often cancel the last measurement they've made on a scale to protect proprietary versions of recipes from their own staff. This is our nature; we have so little that isn't already exhaustively revealed in thousands of cookbooks. So please forgive us this covetousness, and don't be offended if your friend Sally refuses to give you the recipe for her famous apple pie. It is your faux pas for asking her in the first place.

I will, however, faithfully share a cookie recipe that is akin to my signature confection. As a matter of fact, anything I give you here, I'm offering freely and without exclusions. And you'll be happy to know that this particular cookie has a keen following of its own and shares the exact shape as its chewy, almondy sister.

Starry Starry Nights are black with chocolate. Dipped in sugar twice before baking, they take on a complex crackle of shiny white sugar offset by veins of ebony. They are profoundly chocolaty, matching a pure ganache truffle for cocoa value ounce for ounce. But they don't melt and you can freeze them. And, of course, they are baked.

Starry Starry Nights are as much careful process as they are high-quality ingredients. It's easy to cut a corner and court disaster. Pay attention: to the chocolate, to the eggs, to the temperature and feel of your ingredients at every stage. Make sure to have extra chocolate on hand to nibble as you work; it calms the impatient baking beast beautifully.

2 large eggs

2.4 ounces (¼ cup plus one tablespoon) sugar,
plus additional for dipping

1 tablespoon honey

8.2 ounces bittersweet chocolate (I use 2 whole
bars plus 2 strips of bittersweet Lindt
chocolate which comes in a 3.5 ounce/100g
bar and is available in most grocery stores)

3 tablespoons butter

2.6 ounces slivered almonds (about ⅝ cup
slivered almonds measured before grinding)
ground to a fine powder

½ teaspoon salt

1 tablespoon non-dutch processed cocoa
powder

*Baker's Note: To get almond flour, grind almonds
in a food processor until they become a meal,
almost floury, but be careful not to process so
long that the almonds become a paste. You'll need
about 5/8 cups almonds for 2.6 ounces of almond
flour.*

Combine the eggs, sugar, and honey in the bowl of
an electric mixer. Beat with the whisk attachment

on high speed until the mixture reaches a thick ribbon stage.

Melt the chocolate and butter together in a heatproof bowl over simmering water. Cool slightly.

Toss the almond flour, salt, and cocoa in a bowl until well combined. Add to the melted chocolate and mix until fully incorporated.

Add a quarter of the whipped egg mixture to the chocolate to lighten. Stir until no egg is visible. Gently fold the rest of the egg mixture into the chocolate until well combined, being careful to maintain the aerated quality of the eggs.

Chill until firm.

Place a few tablespoons of sugar in a small bowl. Using the smallest cookie scooper available (I use one the size of a melon baller), scoop individual cookies, dip them in the sugar, and place on a parchment-lined sheet pan ½ inch apart. Freeze uncovered until very hard, about an hour.

Preheat the oven to 350°F/180°C. Just before baking, dip each cookie in sugar again. Bake 10 minutes, turning after 5 minutes to ensure even baking. Cookies should be slightly cracked but the sugar should not be browned.

Chapter Six

Eat, Drink, and Be Larry

7 a.m.

W HEN I RETURN FROM THE SOY RUN, I'm on the lookout for Larry's car. He's everyone's favourite regular. If he doesn't come in by 8 a.m., I get worried. But I spy him through the one-way mirror that separates the kitchen from the store, a sticky bun in a take-out bag and a cappuccino in his personal porcelain mug. He's making Bonnie laugh. Jim, Claude, and Jeff sit on the antique bench by the wine refrigerator, nursing their morning lattes. Carol's waiting on her coffee and nibbling on a turnover. She's my doctor; she's seen me naked and knows my cholesterol levels. Beth is watching Lily make her latte, standing patiently by the marble table filled with candies. Wave after wave of familiar faces; most people we know by name. Others we name after their favourite pastry or coffee drink.

If you work with us long enough, you get to know the regulars intimately. Sometimes the relationship deteriorates rapidly, as it often does with Claudette. She demands warm embraces and clings for minutes at a time, whispering to you that she suffers from depression due to the vagaries of her antipsychotic medications and then hands you a bag of fresh dog poop that she's been clinging to during the entire squeeze. Or Ida, the physical ideal of a 'sweet little old lady' who, in reality, is an ornery, racist hellcat. We sic her on the new help to break them in, see how they handle an hour of interrogation and the occasional bigoted aside. 'I hate those Japs, them and their cameras!'

There are the merely strange, like the young woman who insists on loudly complaining about her latest outbreak of forehead herpes, a medical condition she has named Zoroaster. And then there are the simply annoying, the man who approaches the counter midconversation on his cell phone and plants himself at the register with his index finger raised to indicate 'Don't bother me. On a very important call. Will get to you when I'm ready.' Or the guy who takes honey in his coffee every day, and every day approaches the honey dispenser as if it's a contraption he's never laid eyes on before. And breaks it. Or those who ask for their pastries cut into eighths. And Bess, who while waiting for her drink and scone has asked a neighbouring female customer with very short hair whether she's undergoing chemotherapy. She's done this twice.

There's the cream pie guy, a crank caller with whom I unwittingly had phone sex. He called and asked, 'Do you make cream pie?'

'Of course, all kinds.'

He got very breathy. 'What kinds?'

'Oh, you know, all kinds. Coconut, banana, chocolate.'

He got testy. 'But cream pies. You didn't say they were *cream* pies.'

'Well, yeah. I was just listing the kinds I make. Banana, coconut . . .'

'CREAM! You're not saying that they're cream pies! What kind of CREAM pies?'

And I started in again like a moron, 'Okay, banana cream, coconut cream, chocolate cream, devil's cream.'

My new best friend on the other end got quiet.

And then he hung up.

We also cater to the Burl Ives contingency. Montpelier and its environs house an inordinate number of older gents with neatly trimmed white beards. Most of them bespectacled. All of them physically endearing in the nice-old-guy kind of way. And all but a few, leering. I'll be the first to admit that we have some very comely lasses manning the front counter. But I must draw a line when, from the back of the store, I can actually intuit if a member of the contingency is staring at one of our counterwomen's asses too intently. My antidote is to run out front and slam something heavy on the counter.

And then there are the vegans. 'Tell Ja-zeen that she really should make vegan things. Because all this butter and dairy...it's not right and it's not healthy.'

There's a damn fine reason that I'm always in the back baking and rarely up front at the counter with the customers. I'd have whipped off my wood-soled clog and chucked it at that nitwit's head. Because when I hear something like this, someone butchering my name *and* proselytising, I'm ready to throw down.

I've got nothing but love for the vegans. Really. Walking such an ardent and thoughtful path is a beautiful thing. My mom, she lived much of her life a dedicated vegan. She even went above and beyond: growing her own organic produce, using only holistic beauty products, collecting water from a natural spring high up in the Blue Ridge Mountains in a hundred-pound glass bottle and schlepping it back to the suburbs because tap water was toxic. And still she died of colon cancer. Oh. Before she died but after she was diagnosed, she went on an epic bender. She ate everything: dairy, meat, a bag of frozen bite-sized Snickers. Because she was pissed. She'd denied herself for so many years.

Personally, I believe deeply in the need for the humane treatment of our farm animals. I don't think there's any good reason for factory farming. But don't walk into my shop, a clearly marked pastry establishment built on kindness, dairy, and eggs, and pontificate on the evils of my trade. I might suggest taking a trip to France instead. The French invented the cream and butter-logged benchmarks of pastry: éclairs, napoleons, palmiers. They'd *love* to listen to your admonishments. Better yet, take a trip to Tibet and protest their exuberant use of yak butter in everything from candles to cooking.

So you kind people, perhaps you should change your approach from that of arrogance to one of respect. Because all animals, farm and human, deserve as much. Who knows, you may even convert me. But it's doubtful.

Some people come in and treat our place like it's a literary agency/Hollywood studio, dropping off scripts and books for us, assuming that we crank out croissants and films in the back. There are those customers who come in a bit anxious, maybe perspiring strangely. They laugh inappropriately, holding on to an article about the shop, and demand to see me. Specifically, and without fail, they will say, 'Can you bring her out.' It's not a question; it's a statement. As if the blurb about our shop describing my pastries and mentioning my famous sister gives them a ticket to the Gesine petting zoo. They unfailingly butcher my name in the process, sometimes adding that they are on a 'mission from God' in a plea for an audience. For all these folks, we have the blue sticky of doom. It doesn't need to be blue; whatever colour Post-it we have on hand will do. But it always has the same purpose. Whoever's working the counter sticks it on the glass of the door dividing the kitchen from the shop as a clear warning that I should come out at my own risk.

By and large, we have positive relations with our customers, and often we come to love them and look forward to their visits. Marita, who covets vanilla teacakes and Starry Starry Night truffle cookies, is as lovely a human being as you'll ever meet. For her own birthday, she came staggering into the shop with a fifty-pound plaster horned owl lawn ornament she found at an estate sale, a gift for us, just because. It sits high on our lawn, overlooking the path from the house to the barn, greeting me before dawn and at sunset every day. Ann brings us cocktails at close in her vintage shaker during the dog days of summer and the endless baking days of Christmas, lavender martinis to ease a baker's weary bones. We have a beautiful owl print in the shop from Ann. She fought to the death for it at the notoriously cutthroat Christmas Yankee gift exchange.

Little gifts, in the way of kindness, come our way daily. Some of them are life-changing reminders of the intimacy and goodness of our trade. We nourish our neighbours with sweets and caffeine and they reciprocate with graciousness and thanks.

And then there's Larry. Trim, medium height, late fifties, handsomely hawk-nosed and balding. On an average Larry day he enters the shop, not cracking a smile, and gives off a general air of grumpy. If a kid comes in, he'll hand Bonnie some money and tell her that whatever the kid wants, it's on him. He's the lovable curmudgeon you always wished existed but thought you'd see only in the movies. We started getting postcards from Larry a few weeks after we first opened. Little notes of thanks and encouragement. He comes in every day and we still get postcards on the side. He brings daisies and tulips for our birthdays. On the store's first-year anniversary, he walked around town all day with a perfect rendering of our owl logo painted on his bald spot. He brings Ray choice cuts of meat from the farmer's market and will slip a pound of haricot verts fresh from the garden into the kitchen when I'm not looking. If you're new to the shop and Larry's around, you'll find yourself with half of whatever he's eating in your hand, an invitation to try something good, no thanks required. On our store's third anniversary, he brought me the kitschiest clock in history: an owl, flanked by two baby owls, her chest housing the clock face, her eyes moving back and forth to the rhythm of the seconds ticking away. I immediately mounted her on the wall of my workstation. And the one time Ray and I took a week off and left the store open, we arrived in Italy to find a fax at our hotel from Larry: 'Everything's great. Opened on time. Case is full. You're in good hands. Now go and relax.' But try to give Larry a hug or even an effusive thank-you and he returns with a gruff rebuke. His life is otherwise full; we aren't the sole recipients of his generosity. He leaves a snow shovel in the bed of his pickup truck in the wintertime, making paths for strangers where paths need to be made. He has made it a part of his life's work to dole out kindness, and we are very lucky beneficiaries.

Years ago, I'd have been hard-pressed to imagine unbridled generosity from my colleagues, let alone acknowledgement and thanks for my work. And forget finding any deep meaning permeating my working life. I had a very glamorous gig, on paper. I was paid well, I travelled to great places first class, I ate at the best restaurants with muckety-mucks. What kind of dummy checks out of a job like that? I was very happily married to a man who managed to be smart, talented, funny, kind, and handsome and we lived in a house in the Hollywood Hills, with two fuzzy dogs who cleverly evaded hungry coyotes. And I drove around in a hybrid. I never had to stop and get gas.

But it wasn't really glamorous. That's the major misconception about Hollywood; that by virtue of working in its confines you're part of a dazzling cavalcade of joie de vivre and champagne. But if you're a working stiff, an executive at a studio or an independent producer, you're still a 'suit.' Just one who has a few more celebrity sightings than most. And if you're a celebrity chances are, despite your irritatingly good looks, you're pretty normal. Most days for everyone involved in the entertainment industry are just boring. Just spend an hour on a movie set sitting around waiting for a lighting setup that takes half a day and then talk to me about glamour. It doesn't exist.

So in this glitz-free atmosphere, I ran my sister's production company for nine years. We made movies and television shows. She was the world-famous actress who made things happen, and I was her workaday proxy when she couldn't be in ten places at once. I worked with the studio, I worked with the director and writers, and I made sure everyone was working with each other. If you needed something, you came to me to complain that you weren't getting it. And I'd get it. If you had an idea or a script, you'd come to me and ask me to read it. If I liked it, there was a chance it would get made or at least read by someone who had the money to get it made.

One evening I was dining at a massive table at a fabulous New York restaurant. There were eight in our party – a few movie stars, a handful of studio executives, two writer/directors, and me, all of us squirming in our au courant post-industrial tropical wood seating.

I was at the very end, closest to the kitchen. It was the rubberneck's perch usually reserved for a screaming kid's booster seat. I spent much of the evening rocking back and forth trying to get feeling back in my ass and accidentally locking eyes with a manicured gentleman at another table directly in my sight line.

Our host ordered family style for the table, a tidy mound of mashed potatoes whipped with a pound of butter and a quart of heavy cream, shiny pork ribs piled high in a burnished copper sauté pan, flash-fried spinach with tissue-thin slivers of truffle and garlic, a whole roasted guinea hen cosily nesting in roasted fingerling potatoes and caramelised hunks of onion. He'd ordered each dish in triplicate, so that no one had to suffer the stretching and 'would you please' politeness of passing. It turned out that I had a family meal to myself; no one was sitting across from me to share.

We were celebrating. We were days away from shooting a new movie. Now was the perfect time – after the work of preparing to film had finished and before we started rolling camera and screwing up – to party and pretend that everything would proceed flawlessly.

To commemorate the event, our host had proudly emblazoned T-shirts with what he thought was the perfect title for our project and had made one for each of the relevant cogs in the film, a lovely and thoughtful gesture to be sure.

He passed them out with great fanfare. To the writer/directors, to the studio executives, to the movie stars, and when he got to my lonely end of the table, I waited with an expectant and gracious smile, turtleneck snug up to my chin, a piece of guinea hen lodged uncomfortably between my front teeth. But I didn't get a T-shirt. The T-shirt well was dry. I accidentally locked eyes again with my awkward dining companion at the other table and he gave me a sympathetic shrug.

I should have been used to working on projects without anyone giving a shit about what I did. I don't know why I wasted time being insulted. But I was, and now all I wanted was dessert to make me feel better.

I was tired of sulking and feeling like a martyr; I wanted to grow up and stop caring about getting a pat on the back and my very own sweatshop T-shirt. But no one else was going to lead me to fulfilment and happiness. That wasn't anyone's obligation but my own. I had to stop being a spineless weenie. I had to stop complaining and expecting fulfilment from my work and kindness from my colleagues; no one was holding a gun to my head and forcing me to live in Hollywood. Either I had to shut up or move on.

The pastry chef came to our table and placed a small brown bag in front of each of us, saying, 'This is for breakfast or a midnight snack.' I opened the parcel she'd left on the table and took a whiff of warm sticky bun, comfort in a bag, much better than a stupid old T-shirt any day. Like the warm bread and chocolate we had as kids in Germany as a treat for breakfast, sticky buns embody all things that are nurturing in pastry. And with her gift, this pastry chef had given me the answer to my quandary before I'd even asked the question. It just took me a few more years of misery to finally figure that out.

Today, I make sticky buns for a living. It's not always rosy, this life. We make the same things every day; that can get a little monotonous if you're not thoughtful. If we stop, for a single day, we'll get grief from customers. But I don't mind that they use me for my gift; I'm happy to be their pastry slave. And when time is with me and inspiration strikes, I'll dream up something new and spend an hour madly in love with baking, job satisfaction wrapped in instant gratification. You tell me what you're craving and I'll bake it for you. But the joy doesn't lie in the recognition for making the cake; it's the act of making the cake that brings me contentment.

Maple Pecan Sticky Buns

STICKY BUN DOUGH is ravishing; it's shiny, spongy, buttery, and soft. Like other rich yeast doughs, Danish and challah, it starts to rise and you want to hug it and bite it. You really shouldn't. But you can touch it gently and sometimes you have to knock it down, it starts rising so quickly that it spills out of its bowl.

Yeasted doughs take time. They aren't tricky but they require patience. This is the pastry you think about making on snowy Sunday mornings but by the time you wake up and decide to go for it, your brioche won't be ready until dinner. So do what I do in the bakery. Make a batch and freeze them. Then thaw them overnight in the refrigerator and take them out about an hour before you want to bake them to allow them to proof in your cosy kitchen. Brush your little wound pieces of dough on the top and sides with a bit of egg wash and bake them in a 375°F/190°C oven for about forty-five minutes and you're golden.

And play with the recipe. Feel free to use the dough however you like. Use ground pecans and brown sugar for a filling, or make a traditional cinnamon bun. The dough's not going to stop working just because you decide to do something a little different; I won't tell anyone. If this is your first yeast dough, and you like playing with it as much as I do, I suggest you move on to making Danish or challah. Take a dip into making croissants and fill them with chocolate. Be brave but be patient. If you screw up – and you really should a few times if you want to get good – keep trying.

MAKES 12 BUNS

For the starter
1 teaspoon sugar
¼ cup warm milk or water (105°F/40°C)
One ¼-ounce package active dry yeast (2½ teaspoons)
½ cup sifted all-purpose flour

For the dough
¼ teaspoon salt
3 tablespoons sugar
1 tablespoon warm milk or water (105°F/40°C)
2 large eggs
1½ cups sifted all-purpose flour
12 tablespoons (1½ sticks) unsalted butter, softened, plus additional for the bowl

For the syrup

8 tablespoons (1 stick) unsalted butter

1 cup packed light brown sugar

1 cup maple syrup

1 cup chopped pecans

For the filling

1 cup packed light brown sugar

1 cup chopped pecans

1 teaspoon cinnamon

For assembling the buns

8 tablespoons (1 stick) unsalted butter, at room
    temperature

FOR THE STARTER

Combine the sugar and milk in the bowl of an electric mixer. Sprinkle the yeast over the mixture and let stand until foamy, about 10 minutes. Stir in the flour, forming a soft dough. Let the starter rise, covered with plastic wrap, at room temperature until doubled.

FOR THE DOUGH

Combine the salt, sugar, and milk in a small bowl and stir until the salt and sugar are dissolved.

Fit the mixer with the dough hook; add the eggs, sugar mixture, and flour to the starter and mix on low until a soft dough forms. Slowly add 1 stick of the butter and mix until the dough is smooth and elastic, about 6 minutes. Add the remaining butter and beat 1 minute, or until the butter is incorporated.

Lightly butter a large bowl and scrape the dough into the bowl with a rubber spatula. Lightly dust the dough with flour to prevent a crust from forming.

Cover the bowl with plastic wrap and let rise at room temperature until more than doubled in bulk, 2 to 3 hours.

FOR THE SYRUP

In a skillet, heat the butter, sugar, and maple syrup until the butter and sugar melt. Set aside and allow to cool.

FOR THE FILLING

In a food processor, pulse the sugar, pecans, and cinnamon until the nuts are in fine pieces but be careful not to turn the mixture into a paste.

TO ASSEMBLE THE BUNS

Punch down the dough and turn onto a well-floured surface. Gently roll the dough into a 12 by 18-inch rectangle of uniform thickness, preferably at least ¼ inch.

Spread the soft butter that you've set aside over the entire surface of the dough except for the top ½ inch along one long side of the dough. Sprinkle the pecan-sugar mixture evenly over the butter and, starting at the long side opposite the unbuttered ½-inch border, roll the dough like a jelly roll into a log. Pinch the dough along the seam to seal. Using a sharp serrated knife, cut the dough into 12 even pieces.

If you are freezing the buns, place them on parchment paper on a baking sheet, wrap well with plastic, and store in the freezer.

If you're baking them right away, pour the cooled syrup into a half sheet pan and sprinkle with the chopped pecans. Place the sticky buns on top of the mixture, cut side down and evenly spaced, about an inch apart. Let them sit for half an hour to an hour, until puffy. While the buns are resting, preheat the oven to 375°F/190°C. Bake until the tops are golden brown and the syrup is bubbly, about 30 minutes.

Chapter Seven

Ode to the Oreo

8 a.m.

I'M FRANTICALLY STABBING THE SIDE of a plain croissant with a razor-sharp paring knife, making an opening just large enough to shove in three long slivers of bittersweet chocolate. Pop it in the oven at 350°F/180°C for a few minutes, enough time to make it a little melty, and then race out to the front to all but shove it in the gaping maw of the kid who won't let up with the piercing wail. 'I WANT A CHOCOLATE CROISSANT! I WANT A CHOCOLATE CROISSANT!'

Kids, they get cranky when they want sugar. And most kids are pretty specific regarding what will alleviate the whining. Some kids just want a chocolate chip cookie. Don't bother asking if they want a flaky napoleon or a delicate pistachio blackberry vacherin. The little maniac screaming his pants off at the counter clearly had his heart set on a chocolate croissant. So I'm happy to make one on the fly, not just to stop the god-awful racket coming from the front of the store but mainly because I've felt that pain. I went to extreme measures to get my sugar fix.

Until I was five, I lived in Europe except for a few pit stops back in the States that barely registered. I was cared for by my mother, my grandmother Omi, my aunt Christel, and an American nanny named Martha who suffered acute homesickness. Every one of these women fed me. And no one kept notes on who gave me what and when. So, even if my mother wasn't buying into my obnoxious plea for some life-saving gummi bears, I had three other caretakers to shake down for sweets.

When we moved back to the States for good in 1975, Mom was in sole control and she put us on a dietary lockdown of whole-grain, tofu-laced, sucrose-free hell. She did not approve of the sugar-coated, red dye #2-infused, synthetically flavoured pantheon of American food. Every avenue of relief I relied on in Germany to get my fix had vanished in a single eight-hour plane ride across the Atlantic.

And then I met Stacey Coleman. The Colemans lived just across the street from us in a sprawling pea green 1950s ranch house with a pantry stocked with shrink-wrapped and artificially preserved snacks. Stacey Coleman introduced me to her treasure trove of comfort food. One cupboard was dedicated to an array of identically hued orange pasteurised cheese foodstuffs painstakingly categorised into crunchy Cheetos, individually wrapped cheese crackers sandwiching peanut butter, Kraft mac and cheese, and Cheez Whiz. Another was devoted entirely to a psychedelic rainbow of breakfast cereals: Trix, Cocoa Puffs, Cap'n Crunch. The fridge boasted processed lunchmeats, individually wrapped cheese slices, peanut butter and jelly interwoven in a conjugal helix in the same jar. There was Wonder Bread in the breadbox. And cookies. Flimsy cardboard boxes filled with Girl Scout favourites and jars absently crammed with sandwich cookies shaped like peanuts, waffley rectangles, creamy vanilla spheres. And Oreos.

Nothing compared, gastronomically, in my home. We were the whole wheat to her refined white.

Arlington, Virginia, where we finally landed, lies just to the west of the District of Columbia, sharing a small portion of the Potomac River and partaking in all the swampland heat of its summers. My mother refused to turn on the air conditioning unless the mercury rose above 100 and there was a complete lack of breeze. Stacey's house, unsurprisingly, was delightfully refrigerated.

I'd tool by her house slowly, hoping she'd be home and let me in. Once when I was eight, her housekeeper, Betty, took pity on me and invited me to join her for a quick iced tea while she watched her stories and tidied up the kitchen. As I was taking my leave, Betty offered to send me off with a fruity Popsicle to keep me cool on the trip across the street back home. She left the kitchen to get the treat from the garage freezer – long enough for me to see that the cabinet with the stash of Oreos had been left wide open. The entire package fit nicely inside my T-shirt.

Before she could get back I bid a hasty, 'Thanks, Betty, but I hear my mom yelling for me!' and I was out the door, on my bike, and down the street.

The Pattersons, our neighbours across Twenty-sixth Street, had a stately elm with a rickety tree house. Their kids were college age and only used the place to smoke pot in the late summer evenings, so I dumped my bike on the curb and almost made it to the top of the ladder when I looked down and noticed that the Patterson's mailbox was tantalisingly full. So much reading material was crammed into their box that the lid was propped open, giving me a full view of catalogues and manila envelopes containing a promising array of diversions.

I placed my prized cookies in the tree house for safekeeping and rifled through the mail. I took a very large envelope with the words 'Do Not Bend!' carefully inscribed on a diagonal on the front.

Pictures. Perfect. An easier distraction than reading.

I gave the photos (wedding pictures, only two of which contained the Pattersons) a quick glance. The cookies owned the moment. And never having had so much sugar so quickly, I ate them all. I found myself wound tight with energy and aggression so profound that I felt the need to ransack the entirety of our quiet neighbourhood. I tore through the rest of the Pattersons' disappointing mail and tossed the evidence into the storm drain. I pried open the Metzgers' garage and dragged out Lydia's prized toys. I can't recall what it was that I took, but I destroyed it. It ended up in the sewer along with the pilfered mail. I tried fishing out some of the koi in the Stewarts' newly dug pond but only managed to catch my foot on an ornate stone pagoda, knocking it over.

I dragged myself home, slumped onto the couch, and just before my head hit the armrest I remembered the stash.

My mother squirrelled anything worth chewing in the cupboard above the stove, including secret shipments from Germany of chocolate, marzipan, and Nutella. It was a narrow cubbyhole so high and awkward that it took standing on the stovetop and a one-armed pull-up for an eight-year-old kid to reach. I was on Oreo rocket fuel; I had the Nutella jar in my grubby paws inside a minute.

I grabbed the biggest spoon I could find, dug a crater right into the centre, and coated my tongue.

I dipped into the well again and again, consequences be damned. The moment was pure, it was chocolate-covered silence. I began to dance and spin with joy. To be alive and coated with chocolate! As I spun my way into the living room with the hypnotic glee of a cocoa-buzzed dervish, I imagined a life devoid of whole wheat, one brimming instead with sweets. Walls shingled with gingersnaps, mortared together with Nutella, streets paved with Oreos. Ice cream stored in snowdrifts within reach of the front door. Gummi bear seat cushions and chocolate toothpaste. I could see the future and it was good. And then I passed out.

When I came to, I opened my eyes to a view of my mother staring at the silk organza curtains that hung from either side of the living room picture window, Mrs. Patterson standing just behind her. Smack dab in the middle of a panel was what appeared to be a brown slug, clinging for dear life. Being German and unafraid of most things, my mother inspected the creature closely. She sniffed it, poked it, and licked her finger.

'Nutella!' she cried and smacked me. 'Federal mail tampering,' Mrs. Patterson added, for which I got another wallop.

My punishment could have been far worse had my mother discovered the initial theft that sparked my spree. But one vital person kept quiet – Betty. She must have known. She kept that house in such fastidious order that she'd have noted in an instant the absence of an entire family-sized package of Oreos. But she was a kind woman. She knew about the brutal culinary conditions at my home. She did, however, store the Oreos in a much higher cupboard from that day forward.

Watching the kid shoving the makeshift chocolate croissant into his screaming pie hole, I feel a sense of great civic pride. I could very well have stopped this kid from committing a felony. Had he not received his croissant, God knows what he'd have done to fill the emptiness. I know first hand what it is to be denied a treat and the dark places you can go to rectify that injustice.

To be honest, we've created what I dreamed of as a kid. But I also believe that our shop would have been a safe haven for my mother. Because I've grown up just a little, where the sugar bombs no longer hold sway over my chocolate-jimmy-coated heart. I bake everyday remembering what it was like to peer into a pastry case full of insanely cool-looking treats as a kid, only to discover they tasted like crap. But Mom, she baked with a sense of occasion and utter sincerity. She made things that were beautiful and delicious. So, like her, I bake like I mean it in a little store made of all things good. And I'm not the only one who thinks so; we're inundated everyday with like-minded pastry penitents who stand in line for cookies and candies, cakes and pies, and wonderfully strong coffee. I think Ray might even be able to fashion an ice cream cooler from a snowdrift to make the picture complete.

Devil's Cream Pie

THIS IS AN HOMAGE. To America. To the Colemans and their cupboard of cookies. And to the things that are just plain bad for you but that taste so good. So yes, it requires the use of Oreos. I will be brutally honest with you; I am a dessert snob. I bristle when someone orders 'German chocolate cake,' as there is nothing remotely German in filling a chocolate cake with clotted bits of coconut and pecan. I'm strangely offended when anyone asks if I make vegan anything. Really? You want something without butter, cream, or eggs? Stand still while I whip off my wooden clog and chuck it at your scruffy head.

But I am not so uptight that I can't appreciate the beauty in white toast smothered in smooth Jiffy peanut butter and Marshmallow Fluff. There are occasions when only a Ding Dong will do. And yes, Oreos. They make transfat transfabulous.

Devil's Cream Pie is a silk pie. It's a cousin to a chocolate mousse, but the cream isn't whipped and incorporated into the chocolate/custard base, so you don't get a light and airy-textured dessert. This is dense and dark. It's not for the faint-hearted and certainly not for anyone on a regular regimen of beta-blockers.

The topping is light; I use meringue. But feel free to use whipped cream or fresh fruit or both. You can infuse the chocolate with extracts – raspberry, cherry, or mint. You can use milk chocolate or even gianduja, which is a heartbreakingly delicious hazelnut chocolate. But always use the best chocolate you can get your hands on. I use Callebaut semisweet. There is something to this chocolate that is true and pure. Valrhona is another gorgeous chocolate; it imparts a fruitier flavour to the finished product. Lindt chocolate is also fantastic. My grandmother ate Lindt bittersweet chocolate religiously and lived to be ninety. So you can't go wrong there, either.

Use heavy cream. The higher the fat content, the happier you'll be. And of course Oreos.

MAKES ONE LARGE 8-INCH CAKE

For the crust
½ package (18 ounces) Oreos, crushed
½ pound (2 sticks) unsalted butter, melted,
  plus more for the pan (or use nonstick
  spray)

For the filling

2 cups heavy cream

1 tablespoon vanilla extract

2 tablespoons sugar

2 tablespoons unflavoured gelatin

1 cup whole milk

1 pound chocolate, finely chopped (see
   headnote)

For the meringue topping

10 egg whites

2 cups sugar

FOR THE CRUST

Lightly coat an 8-inch springform pan with butter or nonstick cooking spray.

Pulverise the Oreos in a food processor until very fine.

Place the Oreos in a bowl, add half the butter, and mix with a spoon. You don't want the finished product to be wet; you simply want it to hold together when you pinch a bit between your fingers. So go slowly. Often you'll find that you'll need differing amounts of butter to cookie depending on the humidity, so pour and incorporate slowly.

Transfer the butter-cookie mix to the pan and

pat the crumbs so they coat the bottom and the sides of the pan evenly. The sides can be left a little jagged; they don't have to be uniform but they should be well coated with crumbs. Set the crust aside.

FOR THE FILLING

In a heavy saucepan, bring the heavy cream, vanilla, and the sugar to a low boil. Meanwhile, in a shallow bowl, sprinkle the gelatin over the milk and let it sit until it looks completely damp and starts to bloom. To make sure it doesn't clump, sprinkle the gelatin very evenly over the milk, give a quick stir, and give it enough time to soak up moisture from the milk so it looks uniformly wet.

Take the cream off the heat once it reaches a boil and pour in the milk-gelatin mixture. Stir with a whisk to incorporate the gelatin, then immediately add the chocolate. Stir so the hot liquid completely covers the chocolate. Let this sit for a few minutes, then whisk the chocolate, making sure that it is completely melted and combined with the liquid.

Holding a sieve over the crust, pour the chocolate mixture into the sieve so that any unmelted clumps of gelatin are left behind and only smooth chocolate goodness is in your crust. Carefully transfer to the refrigerator and leave until set, uncovered, preferably overnight.

FOR THE MERINGUE TOPPING

You can use powdered meringue for the topping, but I always use fresh egg whites. At a professional bakery, we use pasteurised egg whites. Pasteurisation kills the nasty bacteria. Some grocery stores carry pasteurised egg whites, but make sure you read the label. Some aren't meant for meringue. Eggology is a brand that works really well.

Place the egg whites and the sugar in a mixing bowl and set it over simmering water. Whisk until the sugar is completely melted and the temperature reaches 160°F/70°C. You can use a candy thermometer or a laser thermometer, which is a lot faster and more fun. Whisk briskly and constantly; you're not trying to beat the whites stiff at this point but you do want to make sure they don't start to curdle and turn into scrambled eggs. So it's a little dance, with the thermometer and the whisking, but you'll get it.

Once you've reached temperature and the sugar is melted, quickly transfer the mixing bowl to the mixer fitted with the whisk attachment and start it up on high right away. Just sit and wait. You're making Swiss meringue. (If you add some room-temperature butter to the meringue – a little over a pound – you'll have buttercream. But don't add butter for this. Just be patient.)

Beat until the egg whites are bright white and stiff. By stiff, I mean stiff. If you take the whisk attachment out of the meringue, you'll get a peak that will stay. If it starts to peak and then settles back down into the white abyss, keep whipping. You can use this very boring time to fit a pastry bag with a fun tip. Star tips or rose tips. Just find a big tip to make pointy little peaks all along the surface of the chocolate filling once it has set.

Once you've achieved perfect peakdom, fill your pastry bag with meringue and pipe away on top of the smooth surface of the now firm chocolate filling. Or skip the pastry bag, dump a bunch of meringue on top, and just swirl it around to look like a storm-ravaged ocean. It's hard to make meringue look bad, so don't be too precious.

Now spark up your kitchen torch and brown the meringue just a little. It's true that you can brown meringue under a broiler, but not here. You'll just melt the chocolate filling that took you hours to set and you'll be really pissed off. So either buy a torch, leave the meringue naked and bright white, or just whip some heavy cream and use that instead of meringue. If you use the torch, make sure your kitchen towels, this book, and any loose parchment paper are well out of the way. If the meringue catches on fire, blow it out and then continue, holding the torch just a little farther away. Brown it, don't burn it. And then eat it.

Chapter Eight

Crunchy Clouds

8:30 a.m.

WE HAVE TWO MORNING RUSHES. At 7 a.m. the industrious civil servants are already lined up outside when we open; then between 8:30 and 10 a.m. we get a slow migration of young families. But that's only after weary parents have wrestled their toddlers into shoes and strapped them into strollers. There's nothing like a shot of espresso and adult conversation with a counterperson after a long morning of baby hijinks.

Ray and I don't have kids and I can't imagine fitting any in at this point. I'll be honest; I've got none of that baby lust that consumes some people. Babies: pudgy cheeks, tiny fingers, gassy grins, and fat feet; they all look the same to me. Puppies, on the other hand – give me a puppy and I'm putty.

But baking sweets invites contact with children, so whether I ever intended to have little ones in my life, I do now, and dammit if I don't get along with them better than the adult customers. They always know what they want, how they want it, and when they want it. None of this namby-pamby ordering, 'Oh, I don't know. What do you think I want? Am I in a chocolate or strawberry mood?' I'm not a mind reader, and I don't have the time or desire to analyse your deep-seated food phobias and commitment issues. Kids, on the other hand, don't waste my time. It's a chocolate chunk cookie or it's nothing. Do *not* offer them the mango mousses or coconut-pineapple vol au vents when they said chocolate.

To wit, my young friend Sunny likes three things, in this order: chocolate, strawberries, and white crunchy clouds. I told her that I could make crunchy clouds pink if she liked. Pink is her all-time favourite hue. But she's a kid, so she knows what she likes and how she likes it.

'No, I like 'em white. Like the clouds.'

'This is good,' I think to myself. Good that she doesn't require artificial colours to make crunchy clouds (meringues to us mortals) more interesting. Also good for my hands, because I walk around with my palms festooned in radioactive blues, pinks, and greens whenever I use dye.

And now that I'm starting to connect more with kids, I'm getting uptight about what they eat. I don't mind if they're ingesting sugar once in a while. I think it really does more harm than good to place severe restrictions on kids' diets, as evidenced by my criminal Oreo spree. Moderation, education, and a healthy dose of respect for what you're chewing makes for healthier children, not an all-out ban on sweets.

But because I'm starting to care about the little rats, I have a not necessarily hard-and-fast rule: I don't use artificial dye. I'm a pusher of sugar, butter, and high-octane caffeine, so I'm reticent to add to my already plush lineup of comestible sins. And I'm reasonably confident that the average customer knows what they're in for when they suck down a croissant (about a pound of butter) or an éclair (butter, cream, more cream, and sugar); even the kids can figure it out. But dyes are tricky little bastards. They show up in the most unexpected places, especially in children's products. Many are already banned in Europe. My mother, smart woman that she was, banned them from our lives completely when I was young. She didn't understand why you had to inject something not found in nature that added nothing to the taste. But it was this ban that led me to stare longingly at the Colemans' glorious collection of jewel-toned cereals for hours at a time. Trix and Lucky Charms, how you spoke to me from that pantry shelf.

Ultimately my mom was always right. (Except for that time she refused to pull over, insisting it was impossible that I had to pee again. I really did.) I've read that many artificial dyes are connected to hyperactivity in kids. And the stuff is in everything – almost every packaged food, soaps, toothpastes, shampoos, sodas, macaroni and cheese. I have a harder time thinking of things that don't have artificial dye than things that do.

So I try to do my part, using fruit purées to add a splash of colour when someone wants their pastry colourful and fruity. But, like I said, it's not a hard-and-fast rule. It's pretty hard to make a field of vibrant edible Gerber daisies without a smidge of that colourful toxic juice. Sure, I could use the natural dyes made from vegetable extracts. But I'm not sure that a kid would love biting into a Borscht cupcake whose beautiful fuchsia frosting was tinted with beet extract. So I pick my battles.

If I'm making crunchy clouds for kids, I make them strawberry flavoured and they're naturally pink from the fruit. Or if I use raspberry, they take on a mauvey hue. Mango turns them a warm tropical orange, while blackberry is deep purple. Crunchy clouds floating in a warm pastel haze, brimming with fruity goodness.

But that just addresses dye; there's also fat and

sugar to consider. Kids are consuming vats of the stuff and becoming increasingly obese. I've been accused of aiding and abetting our nation's crash weight-gain diet because of the tools of my trade. I'm a baker. I spin out croissants bathed in butter. Cakes awash in whipped heavy cream. Delicate mousses just dirty with pounds of chocolate. But here's the deal. I'm not fat. No one who works for me is fat. And my customers, they aren't fat. Not even close. Okay, a few, but I'm not taking credit. We live in Ben & Jerry's country. I'll shift the blame to them. And sure, some things get away from us and wander into 'supersize' territory, sticky buns for one. No matter what we do, they always come out the size of banquet plates. But hey, sticky buns were originally a German immigrant creation. I blame the Old World for that one.

And cakes. I can't figure out why, when you put me in charge of three layers of cake, filling, and an outer layer of buttercream, I end up with a behemoth. Every damn time.

A few years ago, my cousin Barbara took her husband Hermann and her seven-year-old son Maxi to Disneyland. They'd been making a small tour of the eastern United States. They stopped by D.C., where they visited our transplanted German aunt Erika. They spent a few days catching the sights in New York. And they ended it all at the happiest place on earth.

That winter, I went to visit them in Germany. We

sat around the dining table, lingering over wine and a little cheese.

Maxi asked, 'Hey, you wanna see our pictures from Disneyland?'

I didn't.

I grew up in America. Cinderella's castle, steamy asphalt, heat-stroked teenagers stuffed into plush costumes. I've seen it.

'Yeah. Why not.' I'm polite. And the kid wanted an excuse to stay up a while longer.

I'll hand it to them; the composition of the shots was unusual. Instead of Maxi standing front and centre with the sights framed behind him, he was always standing off in the great beyond. Grinning like a maniac. Hmmm. Strange what they wasted their camera's memory on.

After the fifth nearly identical photo of Maxi in the nether-distance near no discernible site of note, I saw what they saw, the spectacle they felt compelled to record. Fat people. Not just fat people, but grade-A American ground round fat people. Monumental asses. Cathedral-sized guts. They'd come to the Magic Kingdom and spent their day documenting America's tragic gelatinous descent into grotesque obesity. And to dress it all up with a bow, every last wobbling family wore matching T-shirts. The Germans have nothing to compare to our cavalcade of flab, and they even eat dessert.

On the whole, I don't feel responsible for America's morbid fatness. As a matter of fact, I believe that small shops like mine, where we use local ingredients and bake in small, thoughtful batches, are the key to getting us back on track. I'm not offering anything artificial or potentially radioactive, like the stuff that allows industrial, shrink-wrapped piles of sucrose to loiter on grocery shelves for millennia. What we do is so personal to everyone who walks in the shop that there's no disconnect between the pastry and the person. I refuse to look at my work, at my confections, as products, units to be pumped out with increasing rapidity and economy. That's the stuff that's making our kids fat, the value sacks of partially hydrogenated evil.

My German family, they eat pastries almost every day. They stop by their local confectioner midafternoon. Or they bake a tart, brew a fresh pot of coffee, and sit down at 3 p.m. to relax and indulge just a little. It's not that they've forgone treats for the sake of svelte; they just buy and enjoy their treats thoughtfully. That's what I see here, at our shop. One of our regulars, Claude, gets a scone every day. He's lost over fifty pounds since we opened. I've noticed the same kind of conscious consumption at the dwindling small pastry shops around the States. When kids have the experience of choosing something from a pastry case and knowing that the little tart they're going to take home was baked today, just a few steps from where they're standing, they'll savour that small treat, instead of thoughtlessly devouring the entire contents of an economy-sized Acme brand bag of cookies.

Just last week I was driving home and passed two kids on the side of the road, selling lemonade. I made a U-turn and hopped out. They poured me a glass, I paid them a dollar, and I complimented their tart, not-too-sweet homemade nectar. Their mom popped out of the house and said, 'Hey? Are you Gesine?' I was wearing a store shirt.

'Yeah!'

And then she addressed her kids, 'Hey guys, do you know who this is? This is the owl lady. She's the baker!'

I couldn't have been more pleased, because they looked absolutely tickled by the news that they were meeting the owl baker lady. And they were svelte little buggers, lanky active kids who got treats at my shop. I've added them to my growing collection of kids I like and I'm looking out for.

Raspberry Meringues

YOU CAN'T GET AWAY from the sugar in a meringue. People keep asking if I can make them sugar free because that would make the ultimate diet dessert. Sadly, artificial sweeteners can't provide the chemical compounds that the real stuff does, so they don't hold the structure that meringue requires. The sugar's there to stay because you can't change the ratio of egg white to sugar without ruining the whole thing. But I like to tell myself while I'm scarfing twenty of these puppies that they're fat free. And unlike, say, most marshmallows and cotton candy, meringues have egg white. So that's protein – a fat-free protein. And then I get a sugar headache.

MAKES 15 MERINGUES

5 large egg whites, at room temperature
¼ teaspoon salt
¼ teaspoon cream of tartar
¼ cup raspberry purée (I use Boiron. Many high-end groceries carry these purées in the freezer section.)
1 cup sugar

Preheat the oven to 225°F/110°C. Place the egg whites, salt, cream of tartar, and about half of the purée in the bowl of an electric mixer fitted with the whisk attachment. Beat on high until soft peaks form. Gradually add the sugar in a steady stream and continue to beat until the meringue is stiff and glossy. This can take awhile, especially when it's humid. So be patient. If the colour isn't quite as you'd like it, slowly add more purée, but make sure the extra liquid doesn't damage the stiffness of the egg whites.

Line a baking sheet with parchment paper. Place the meringue in a pastry bag fitted with a large star tip and pipe rose-shaped dollops, about ¼ cup each, on the parchment. Bake until dry, 1 to 1½ hours.

Chapter Nine

The Monster on the Wall

9 a.m.

KALIKA, OUR AFTERNOON BARISTA, sticks her head in the kitchen. 'There's someone named Amy here to pick up a cake?'

'What cake? What kind of cake? Where's the order? I don't know anything about a cake for Amy.'

The behemoth wall calendar is nailed just above the phone and the punch clock. There are hundreds of order slips plastered all around, just barely clinging to the calendar with scraps of tape. Each date only has a few inches of real estate, so we have to stick orders on top of each other, creating ominous fans of accountability. As the week wears on, the stacks get progressively sinister until we hit Saturday and the buggers swarm that coveted two-inch square marking Saturday's space. On holidays, we dump the 'tape and pray' scheme altogether and break out a three-ring binder to wrangle all the orders.

But today's an average Tuesday and we're in the hands of the monster on the wall. And it appears that, as it will once in a while, a scrap of paper with young Sammy's birthday cake order – the one Amy is now here to pick up – has unglued itself from its brothers and sisters and gone into hiding in the radiator or is stuck to the underbelly of the workstation. Or maybe someone completely forgot to put the order up, and that likely villain is yours truly. It's been unanimously agreed that I shouldn't be allowed to answer the phone, not only because I'm in possession of barely rudimentary phone etiquette ('Hurry up and just tell me what you want! Chocolate or vanilla, it's not that hard!'), but also because I can't bring myself to post an order once I've taken it. I leave it in the little booklet instead of posting it on the calendar, forgetting it the second I've hung up the phone and hear the oven buzzer screaming in the background or realise the whipped cream is just about to spin itself into butter. Or sometimes I'm sure I'll remember. And I do, in a fashion. Like the time I arrived at a wedding with the five-tiered colossus a day early. Or the fifty-pound baby shower cake, complete with pregnant belly and breasts.

I got the flavour right but the event wrong. It was supposed to be for an eighty-ninth birthday celebration. So I spent a very frazzled ten minutes performing an emergency C-section and double mastectomy on poor Great Aunt Tula's strawberry dream cake.

'Kalika, go ask them exactly what the order was and if it could be under another name. Ask if someone named Jenny could have called it in. I've got a cake for Jenny.'

And we wait and pray. Please, please, please be under another name. Or at least be really nice and understanding and have the time to come back in the afternoon, by which time I will have busted out the cake of Sammy's dreams.

But this is only an occasional drama. I mostly get it right. And when I'm getting it right, I'm in a giddy trance. There's nothing quite like being entrusted with making someone happy. Birthdays, weddings, anniversaries, bon voyages, baby showers – I get to make beautiful and tasty sculptures for strangers every day.

Often it's the order that doesn't mark anything in particular that inspires me. A woman once came to the shop and asked for a chocolate mousse. She asked by way of scribbling on a notepad because she wasn't able to speak. I made her mousse. She took it home. A day later she came back and ripped a page out of her notepad.

'Dear Gesine, I have throat cancer. I've been on a feeding tube for five years and just had it removed. Your chocolate mousse was the first thing I've eaten in all that time and it was everything I could have wished for. It was truly wonderful. Thank you.'

Most of the time when I look at an order it follows the usual guidelines. The top line has the name and phone number of the customer. Then a brief description of the cake and how big it should be. And then there's usually an instruction on what should be written on the cake: 'Happy Birthday!' 'Congratulations!' 'Transformation is good!' (Honest to god, I didn't make that one up.) But when there's no inscription, just a dessert, I've come to wonder what it is that I'm catering to. It could be a childhood memory or a nagging hormonal craving behind the order. A woman called in a few days ago and asked me to put aside six of my daily crop of vacherin, two pistachio meringue cookies that sandwich a tangy layer of blackberry buttercream. She was just about to give birth and came in on the way to the hospital, intent on taking them with her to the delivery room come hell or high water. Or it could be someone's first bite of solid food in five years. It's a mystery and a weighty honour to bake these things.

There have been orders that have brought me to tears.

An older gentleman came into the shop and asked whether I could make a dessert he'd had in Germany during the Second World War. He described a sweet, almost shortbready crust lined with elegant, oval plums that he'd never seen outside of Europe. His wife had recently passed away, he was newly retired, and he was now prone to reminiscing. He wanted to treat himself to a past pleasure and bathe himself in memories through that little plum tart.

Every summer since my mother died, the thought of smelling baking plums and watching the green-fleshed fruit start to bleed red into the buttery dough was depressing. We'd eaten *zwetschgendatschi* every summer we had together – in Nürnberg, in our suburban house in Virginia, and at my aunt's home in Maryland. We bought it from local village bakeries in Bavaria or baked it ourselves.

On the day my mother dropped me off at college, five years after my sister had left, Mom faced the prospect of returning home to an empty nest, and the only thing that could vaguely lift her spirits was a *zwetschgendatschi*. She called late in the afternoon to check on me. She sounded terribly sick. Not just sad but bellyaching and full of binge regret. She confessed that she had stopped at Giant Supermarket on the way home and purchased a five-pound sack of all-purpose flour, a small bag of sugar, two pounds of butter, and a carton of eggs. In the produce aisle she inspected the Italian prune plums, sorting through them until she had collected seven pounds of the finest stone fruit.

In her tidy kitchen, she cut a small knob of butter and greased a sheet pan in efficient strokes. She kneaded the rest of the butter until it was pliable and incorporated it bit by bit into the flour and sugar by rubbing it between her fingertips until it transformed into something resembling cornmeal. She added two eggs, a scant bit of salt, and a touch of vanilla, mixed until a loose dough came together in her hands, and turned it out onto a 14 x 18-inch sheet pan. She pressed the dough into the corners and patted the remainder into an even layer covering the full surface of the pan. While that chilled, she washed the plums gently with a soft, damp towel, split them lengthwise with a razor-sharp paring knife along their natural seam, and pried them open so the pit lay exposed. She expertly manipulated the stone so it popped out cleanly without marring the surrounding flesh and cut a quarter-inch slit at the peak of each half. She made short work of the rest.

She lined the halved plums side by side atop the cool dough, a seven-pound standing army of the empress of plums ready for a sprinkling of sugar and a short trip to the oven. For forty-five minutes she waited. She stood on the back porch and let the Virginia heat have its way with her painstakingly hot-rolled hair. And then she ate the whole damn thing.

When my mother was terminal with cancer and no longer able to leave bed, she had an appetite for only four things. Poached eggs, fillet of sole, red wine, and *zwetschgendatschi*. Sandy took the lead with the fish, Dad kept the red wine in stock, and I had the eggs. But at the time, Italian plums weren't in season; it was March, and I didn't have the heart to make the tart without her. I went, instead, to a lovely French bakery in Georgetown, just across Key Bridge and minutes from our family home. They made a great apricot tart – same idea, different fruit. Each time I walked into the patisserie, I marvelled at the lovely space and allowed myself a few minutes away from the aching sadness and helplessness that comes with watching someone you adore die. But I had to face the tart eventually, now the very symbol of hopelessness, and bring it home to my mother.

Today I have my own patisserie and I'm the baker responsible for the emotional pastry needs of my patrons, like the older man who, along with whatever else he carried home from the war in Germany, had a lasting memory of the pastry that most reminded me of my mother. So I set about making the dough, an industrial mixer replacing my mother's steady hands. I efficiently slice the plums, line them up in a fancy round fluted tart pan, sprinkle them with sparkling granules of sanding sugar, and walk away. None of that homey rusticity of a sheet pan of plums dusted with regular sugar. Nothing sentimental, sad, or remotely reminiscent of death about this task. No sir. Just a professional pastry chef making pastry. Slip the tart into the sterile convection oven. Set the timer. Walk away. Take it out when time's up. Start weeping.

For all of my emotional precautions, that smell conjures my mother. Through the rush of steam I see her strong jaw, her impossibly high cheekbones, kohl-rimmed eyes, and whippet-thin body. I imagine her bringing out two settings of my favourite of her Rosenthal china, smoky blue rings lined on either side with gold just along the edge of translucent porcelain. I set the tart on a serving platter as Mom briskly whips heavy cream by hand. She'll take a seat on the edge of the couch and I'll plop on the worn Persian rug by her side. We'll scoop mounds of luxurious cream on top of the plums and watch the red juices bleed into its stark whiteness and perfume it with musky sweetness. We'll sneak a bit into our coffee. This is what she called 'vacation'. Where she'd take a break from her strict dietary constraints and enjoy an hour filled with sweetness. This is what we shared since I was old enough to be trusted with the good china and until the last day when she was too weak to be able to use it herself.

And even though my eyes are full of tears and my nose is beginning to run ferociously, no condition in which to bake properly, I have to start over and make it as my mother and grandmother would. I want to pay homage to the women who taught me to love the feel of dough and appreciate a fruit so briefly in season. I make another batch of dough but I do it by hand. I slice open each plum and gently poke at the flesh to release the pit, remembering my mother's gentle hands. I cut a notch at the top, holding the paring knife with my thumb resting along the black handle as she did and position each plum just so. While the second tart bakes, I eat the first. It tastes of simplicity, sunshine, and hope, not a bit of sadness or despair.

My mother's youngest sister, my Tante Erika, came to visit the shop not long after this. *Zwetschgen*, the plums, were still in season, and I made Ray drive the hour to Burlington to get them. It was only fitting that I'd make her some. When she arrived and I showed her the tart, she was at once elated and heartbroken. It was her birthday, and my mother had always made her a *zwetschgendatschi* for her birthday. I never knew. It was a ritual shared between two German sisters in America, a celebration of love and homesickness. And with my mother gone, this comfort was forever lost but for a few hours in Vermont when I had unwittingly re-created their time-honoured tradition, only without my mother and with a tart that couldn't hold a candle to hers.

Everything I make has the possibility of becoming someone's *zwetschgendatschi*. An edible succour that can numb an aching heart, help you remember fading fond memories, or create new ones. And sometimes I get calls of thanks. A bride called me the other morning after her wedding to thank me for the beautiful wedding cake. I didn't ask why she was calling the baker instead of engaging in traditional honeymoon hijinks. More often I get little notes tucked into my mailbox or small gifts of thanks.

I'm pretty sure that if I get Sammy's birthday cake out in time, he'll be thanking me and remember his cake well into adulthood with great affection.

Zwetschgendatschi

MY MOTHER MADE a theatrical first impression, her hair perfectly coiffed and teased, rouged cheeks, and crimson lipstick. She wore fake eyelashes in the daytime. She showed up at PTA meetings in stilettos and couture. It is testament to her real beauty that she never came off as a tart but as a glamorous opera diva come to slum it in the suburbs.

But when it came to the grand gesture, expressions of love, affection, and discipline, Mom practiced the powerful art of simplicity. Daisies, not roses. A quick and painful smack on the ass, not time-outs or an 'I'm disappointed in you.' And zwetschgendatschi, not a frilly mousse.

The spirited flavours of this plum tart should never be burdened with anything more than a simple crust and Empress plums. And with a fruit so beautiful and fleeting, it would be criminal to make it compete for attention. Apricots are another fruit that lend themselves nicely to this modest preparation, and they can be substituted for Empress plums if there's nothing else to be had. My only caveat is that you make this with utter sincerity. If you're looking to make the show-stopping crowd pleaser, the shock-and-awe of dessertdom, don't even think about sniffing around zwetschgendatschi. This is the stuff of true love, never boastful or conceited. Bake and serve accordingly.

MAKES ONE LARGE TART

For the short dough
¾ cup sugar
14 ounces (3½ sticks) unsalted butter
1 large egg, well beaten
1 teaspoon vanilla extract
3½ cups all-purpose flour
1 teaspoon salt
Nonstick cooking spray

For the plum filling
3 pounds Empress plums (also known as Italian
    prune plums)

Sanding sugar (optional, available at some gourmet shops and most cake supply stores)
Whipping cream
Place the sugar, butter, egg, and vanilla in the bowl of an electric mixer and beat on low speed with the paddle attachment.
Add the flour and salt; mix just until smooth.

(If overmixed, the dough is hard to work with, so keep careful watch.)

Press the dough flat on parchment paper, cover with plastic wrap and refrigerate until firm, about twenty minutes.

While the dough chills, prepare the plums. Split each one along the natural seam and remove the stone, leaving the plum still hinged on the backside like a little book. Cut a ¼-inch notch at the top of the plum, where the stem was. Why? Because that's how my mother and grandmother did it, that's why . . .

Spray an 8-inch tart pan with nonstick spray. Preheat the oven to 350°F/180°C.

Once the dough has sufficiently chilled (it should be cool to the touch but not rock hard), gently roll it out on a floured surface. Transfer to the prepared pan. Short dough breaks easily, so bits may come off in the transfer from table to pan. No worries. This is the kind of dough where you can take an errant piece and just press it into place without anyone knowing the difference.

For most tarts you'd dock the dough (prick holes all over it), fill it with pie weights or dry beans and bake until the dough has browned a bit before adding the filling. Zwetschgendatschi is different – you arrange the plums upright on the uncooked dough, flesh side facing in. Arrange them in circles, the little plum books open and fit tightly together. In the end you'll have a beautiful tart that looks more like a summer bloom than a dessert.

Sprinkle with sanding sugar if you like. Many people sprinkle extra bits of the short dough on top of the plums like a crumble.

Bake until the sides of the dough are golden brown and the plums are tender, about 45 minutes. Depending on the temperature of your oven, the plums may begin to brown too quickly on top. If this happens, cover the tart lightly with a piece of aluminium foil and continue baking until the crust browns evenly. The crust along the bottom will always be moist from the blood-red juices that weep from the plums.

While the tart cools, make some fresh coffee. Whip a bit of heavy cream by hand, spoon some on the tart, and share it with someone you love.

Chapter Ten

End It with a Sigh

10 a.m.

'GESINE'S. How can I help you?'

'Gesine?'

'Yup. This is she.'

Bear witness to a miracle. I never cop to my identity when I answer the phone at the shop. It leads to avenues of small talk for which I have no patience. And the best way to test my patience is to mispronounce my name. Straight off. After I've just answered the phone and pronounced it.

'Gesine's, how can I help you?'

'Is this Jazeen's? The bakery?'

'Yes, this is Geh-see-neh's. How can I help you?'

This is where I raise the stakes. The first time, fine. No one's really listening when you first answer the phone. Can't expect them to pick up on the pronunciation straight off. So I take my time, releasing each syllable slowly. Putting the full *hochdeutsch* spin on it, staking a claim in the integrity of my name and asking the caller to take the hint and respect it, and at the very least, to try not to malign it again.

'Great. Am I *speaking* to Jazeen?'

'She's not in. Can I help you with anything?'

Say it right, with the hard g and the soft s, and release the last e with a sigh (more of an 'eh' than an 'ah,' but if you get this far, I'll accept either), and I'm putty. But just because the conversation started well thanks to the mellifluous sound of my name done right doesn't mean that the rest of the conversation is going to please me.

'It's Carol.'

Carol, my doctor and a regular. By regular, I mean every morning at 7 a.m. and most afternoons. She gets a small cherry pie every Friday – pie day. I save a cherry turnover if I ever get around to making them. She's a regular's regular.

'About the cherry pie I got today. I think I prefer, even if it means less cherry, a less congealed filling. Maybe less cornstarch or something.'

'I know exactly what you mean. Thanks for telling me. Consider it fixed.'

Rookie mistake. Bush-league baking. Utter nitwittery on a huge scale. It breaks my heart that I let something like this slip.

And this is what really sucks – I didn't make it. Not this time. I've screwed up plenty. Too salty, under baked, too sweet, kept in the freezer to set too long and still frozen when served. It happens and it's the end of the world every time. But worse than screwing up personally, where I can look back and identify the boneheaded mistake and fix it forevermore, is entrusting someone else to help. And then they screw it up. Because it's still my mistake; it's my shop. My standards. My fault. My shame spiral from which it will take a day to recover.

Do I have to do everything? Am I allowed to sleep? Ever? And what if my dog gets sick? What if Inu, my wonder Frisbee dog, suddenly stops catching the disk on the left side, behaving as if it's disappeared into the ether, only to find out he's gone blind? This happened. And the other side's going too unless I drive the four hours to Rhode Island immediately to get his retina skewered into place! Somebody else is going to have to make the cherry filling.

And so it goes, an innocent call setting off a spate of record-breaking nihilism that illuminates just how precarious the whole operation is. The winter of 2007 was the prizewinner for misery. I was holding on to my sanity by a filament of spun sugar. Ray was out of town working in Hollywood all season. But he filled the void with a new puppy. To add to this bounty, we were in the seventh year of a seven-year storm cycle. Every seven years, it snows a lot. It snows a lot every winter in Vermont. The winter of 2007, by December, I couldn't see out of the first-floor windows of our house. Snow kept piling on, foot after powdery foot. The path to and from the house to the barn turned into a fun-house slide; the roads were even worse. If you scream bloody murder at 4 a.m. fishtailing out of your driveway and skid to a stop buried in a snow bank in the woods, can anyone hear you? Apparently not.

Around this time, Tim slipped and broke his collarbone. Tim wasn't just helping me bake. He was doubling as our dishwasher. We actually had a dishwasher. She was lovely. Just a little developmentally challenged. She was in a program whose aim was to give her independence, and we wanted to help. So a few hours before she came in, Tim did the dishes, leaving a handful behind. She came in for a few hours, washed about ten things, and left. Tim and I would carry the dirty dishes we'd been hiding to the sink and he finished the rest. So now I was the dishwasher too. I was not sleeping.

Between the baking, the dishwashing, and the Shetland-sized puppy that used me as a mattress, I was a mess. Perhaps it wouldn't have been so depressing if we were making money at the shop. But we weren't.

The snow and the economy kept everyone at home. Our entire town saw a 20 per cent decrease in business. Everyone talked about shutting their doors. And I missed Ray, but considering the financial pit we were in, he'd have to keep working on films to pay the mortgage.

We're finally digging out of the financial disaster from that winter, but a tax bill could still arrive and erase every cent we have, just when we thought we could actually pay our vendors. Maybe ourselves. Or my favourite mixer gets fried. The water heater explodes. A customer trips outside the shop and breaks her arm. A cherry pie is gummy. Someone finds a washer in a pastry. It's time for Ray and Gesine's monthly conversation entitled 'How much longer can we do this?'

The potential lawsuit, this is something my aunt, Tante Erika, brought up first thing. She's an extraordinary baker. I still ask her to send me Christmas cookies when I'm knee-deep in holiday baking. But when I told her I was opening a pastry shop, something that I thought would appeal to her immeasurably, her initial reaction was to bring up the potential danger I might inflict. A hair. Salmonella. Random body part.

I'd witnessed class-action lawsuits in the making firsthand at the Vermont Venture Center. Large-scale pie makers found a bolt in their pie dough. It came from the ten-ton rotary mixer hidden in the back room behind the walk-in cooler. They found the bolt before they'd filled the pie, packaged it, or sold it, so crisis averted. Until they realised that there was a washer missing as well. And upon closer inspection of the equipment, they noticed a few other bits that weren't accounted for and may or may not have been party to this metal exodus. Or they could have escaped in an earlier batch of dough that had already been shipped and was just biding its time in a supermarket freezer until Grandma takes it home, bites right into it, and shatters her jaw.

I remember thinking quite clearly, this won't happen to me. I'm in control of everything, every ingredient, every piece of equipment. I'm a small-scale operator and anal-retentive. I'm better, smarter, more together, less stoned; I've got higher standards. I'll get my own space with shiny new equipment and I'll do it perfectly.

But a customer did find a washer in an otherwise beautifully executed vacherin one day. We'd been open almost two years and I already had a string of minor disasters behind me. But this was dangerous. And I discovered that no matter how perfectly I think everything is going, equipment doesn't always give you a heads-up when it's about to implode.

I could have killed someone. Our customer brought in the washer and reassured us that no one choked. No teeth were broken. But there it was nonetheless.

Just keeping standards unbearably high, baking like you really mean it every single day, is exhausting. I'm sick of making macaroons. I won't make them everyday. I just won't. You can't make me. There are days that I dread making Danish. The day-long process of making the dough, making the fillings, rolling the dough with painful precision, and measuring and cutting and then starting all over again. And I loathe carrot cake. For a year, Tim couldn't make carrot cake without adding a tear of despair to the batter. Cakes fell for no apparent reason at random intervals. We endured an entire year of sheet pan after sheet pan of cratered cakes. And then Tim slipped on that fresh patch of ice outside while getting blueberries, and was out for six weeks. I inherited the accursed carrot cakes. One day I figured it out, the mysterious reason behind the sudden failure of what once was a perfect recipe: we weren't putting in enough carrot. After years of peeling, cutting, grating, and then rechopping batch after batch of carrots, we'd got progressively lazier and started using less and less carrot until we'd reached a point where the cake protested. 'Screw you guys! I'm not working with you until you give me back my carrots.'

You add to these small annoyances lack of sleep, taxes, vendor bills, health inspector visits, and wild card employees, and my dream bakery turns into a shop of horrors.

The week after Carol called to gently complain

about her gummy pie, I made everything myself. Hundreds of little pies, some with ruby red cherries and hand-braided lattice crusts, double-crusted caramel apple with a sprinkling of shiny sanding sugar, and wild blueberry with buttery sweet crumbles. When the cherries boiled, I added the perfect amount of cornstarch slurry to stiffen the juices and keep it from being runny. When I folded the butter into the pie dough, I knew when I'd finished my last turn that the crusts would be at their ultimate flakiness. I filled the case with my pies and I set aside a cherry to give to Carol, to apologise for the week before and to prove that I was true to my culinary word and reputation.

Lily poked her head back into the kitchen. 'The pies look particularly beautiful today. And Carol said it was the best cherry pie ever.'

That's exactly what I wanted to hear. What's bittersweet is that I want to hear it everyday; I want to be creating nonstop brilliance. Small and large misfortunes keep it from being a constant reality. But I'll keep trying because the beauty of a well-made pie is as close to magic as hearing my name pronounced with the perfect sigh on the last syllable.

Cherry Filling

YOU CAN USE THIS cherry filling for everything from pie and turnovers to Danish. It's simple and filled with summer's promise. Use sour cherries; they're just better. And frozen cherries are perfect. I've added sugar to ensure you don't make ugly pucker faces while you're eating. While you're at it, use another fruit. Raspberries, blackberries, blueberries – they all work. And it won't be gummy. Honest.

   1 cup sugar
   3 tablespoons cornstarch
   ¼ teaspoon salt
   5 cups whole pitted sour cherries or dark sweet
      cherries (about 2 pounds whole unpitted
      cherries)
   1 teaspoon fresh lemon juice (if using sour
      cherries) or 3 tablespoons fresh lemon juice
      (if using dark sweet cherries)
   Butter, optional

Whisk the sugar, cornstarch, and salt in a medium bowl to blend. Stir in the cherries and lemon juice.
   Add your filling to a pie crust as you would

apples to the apple pie recipe or a square of puff pastry that you'll fold into a triangle for a turnover. But before you cover the cherries with dough and bake, dot them with a few bits of butter for an extra hit of yummy. Bake at 350°F and enjoy.

Chapter Eleven

Doing Lunch, the Vermont Way

11 a.m.

LUNCH IS BUSY AND NOISY. We start service at 11 a.m. and keep churning out sandwiches until 3 p.m. But the bulk of our orders come first thing; Vermonters being a conservative dining bunch, they take all their meals early. Tim mans the panini grill and completes pastry odds and ends during lulls. I finish up special cake orders for pickup in the afternoon and start elements for multidimensional pastries that I'll have in the case tomorrow. Opera cakes, alternating layers of moist almond cake, mocha buttercream, chocolate ganache, and marzipan; chocolate pavé slices, five thin layers of spongy soufflé cake sandwiching rich and fluffy chocolate pastry cream, covered with chocolate glaze and decorated with white dots of confectioners' sugar; and Mozart kugel cakes, small domed almond cakes filled with a chocolate truffle and set atop a round of pistachio meringue, covered with pistachio paste, and then doused with a thin layer of chocolate and sprinkled with bright green bits of ground pistachio. These are work-intensive little cakes and they leave the building almost instantly once they hit the pastry case; I feel as if I never made them. But there is an incomparable satisfaction in arranging each meticulously made element so the flavours are balanced and the cake itself is a work of art. This is what I do for lunch these days. Nibbling on pistachios along the way, sneaking into the back office for a few minutes to eat a bowl of yogurt and noodle around on the Internet.

Lunch used to be onerous for me. In Hollywood you 'do' lunch, you don't eat it. There's no savouring or lingering. Instead it's an hour devoted to kissing someone's ass or someone kissing yours. There's little to no eye contact. Your luncheon partner, while keeping up a steady stream of superlatives regarding your latest project and touting his own, keeps his sights on the entrance to check out who's coming in next.

I once had a lunch meeting on Sunset Boulevard. I gave the hostess the name of my dining companion, who'd made the reservation, and she sat me at a table with an aging tanning booth veteran with spectacularly white teeth and a brow that had been recently pulled surgically tight. He moved his man-purse so I could sit. He looked confused. I probably did too, since the agent I was supposed to be having lunch with sounded a bit younger on the phone. And agents usually don't carry man-purses or lunch in leisure suits. No matter. I introduced myself and he jumped right in. My dining companion had a bevy of projects to pitch. My God they were rank, but he just kept on peppering me with crap idea after crap idea, hoping something stuck. He kept it up with verve, his delivery straight from the old school. No apologies and plenty of sparkle. Then the hostess approached our table and very apologetically said, 'I'm so sorry, Ms. Bullock. I sat you at the wrong table.'

Without missing a beat, my new friend whipped out a business card from his man-bag and bid me adieu. 'Call me! We'll do lunch for real next time!'

Seated at the right table with the appropriately fresh-faced agent, he jittered like an inbred lapdog and noodled with his BlackBerry under the table. But his sales pitch was identical to the one I'd just heard at the wrong table. An endless stream of crap film ideas, except that the seventy-year-old plastic surgery victim gave it a little more oomph. This is what I could expect from lunch for the rest of my life: a wimpy salad, tap water, and the same bad pitch. And I couldn't be sure that when it was my turn to sell an idea, it was any better. I couldn't tell any more. Quite honestly I didn't care.

And then I had a lunch meeting the day after one of my worst nights. It was a lunchtime pitch at a studio with another producer I'd worked with and liked well enough. She was a big fish and she was smart. She was tough to talk to on the phone, though. She was always inhaling something, tobacco or weed, so conversations were punctuated with an asthmatic inhalation and luxuriant exhalation, taking up precious minutes I could be spending looking up cake recipes on the Internet. In person, she was a muscled crumb of a woman, a pinch over five feet. She favoured brief skirts, allowing her toned legs free rein to contort. Mostly she pretzelled herself into a lotus position, skirt bunching up around her hips, panties exposed to the world. She was agile enough to torture herself into position and still keep hold of a lit cigarette.

We met a writer; he was pitching an idea. He suffered from a slight nervous palsy and dropped a few pages from his densely packed story outline. We had lunch brought in and we wrestled with the little plastic tubs of salad dressing while we chatted. Pitches always start with cocktail conversation. A little weather, some gossip, a lament on the ever-increasing traffic, and then a slight dissertation on the need for fuel conservation and a switch to smaller, more fuel-efficient cars. Our writer cut off the small talk and jumped straight into his pitch, ignoring his egg salad sandwich. He stumbled into his introduction, stopped and started a few times getting into the rhythm of his story. I tried to chew quietly, afraid any sudden noise would spook him and screw up his concentration.

He gave us a brief synopsis of a heartfelt and politically salient tale and segued into a story that had influenced his opus. It was here that he lost track of his agitation and fell into his natural cadence for storytelling.

'I married a first-generation Chinese American. Her mother lived with us but didn't speak a word of English, so we cobbled together a primitive sign language. A lot of pointing, a little pushing, and vigorous nods. But it was in the kitchen that communication became effortless. She and I cooked together. She taught me generations' worth of her family's recipes, sharing with me a deep history and creating a true kinship. There was eloquent meaning in her gestures that I perfectly understood; we had no need for imperfect translators. We understood each other beautifully in the kitchen. She taught me how little I knew about what we consume and how artless and distant food can be in America. We had our closest moment one day while making dumplings.'

It's rare to get insight into a colleague's life, especially a genuine glimpse devoid of name-dropping and ego stroking. It's a singular experience to witness even a calculated unveiling of vulnerability, so this guy's humble tale of cross-cultural familial intimacy and his realisation that he had a lot to learn from a little old Chinese lady he had heretofore probably looked upon as a cute stereotype was beguiling. That is, until the pretzel-bent producer yelled, 'OH MY GOD! I LOVE DUMPLINGS! There's this fabulous place downtown, you know what I'm talking about, don't you?'

And she nattered on and on, interrupting a lovely story well told by a man who clearly had difficulty speaking naturally in public. I marvelled at the disconnection and self-absorption that had just suffocated the room, this woman compulsively indulging in every urge to talk about herself, the writer scrambling to get his thoughts together, and looking for the right moment to jump back in. And me, just watching it all play out, not trying to help him, not trying to shut her up, guilelessly rubbernecking at the train wreck in front of me and feeling ashamed at my utter lack of interest in steering this pitch back on course. It wasn't the worst thing that had ever happened after ten years in Hollywood, not by a long shot, but it was one of the last things. It was the proverbial straw and I was the camel.

Afterward, walking between the soundstages on the studio lot, dodging golf carts in high heels, I fished my car keys from my bag and folded my legs into my fuel-efficient clown car. I sat with my forehead pressed against the steering wheel, descending into lunacy as I endlessly repeated, 'I hate this place. I hate this place. I hate this place.'

I had started out in the business with so much enthusiasm and hope. But each year most of my promising projects never made it out of development hell, and a slew of other producers' regurgitated schlock made it to the big screen instead. Each year, I wrestled with the knowledge that no matter how well I did my job, no one looked at me as anything but 'her sister' with nothing to offer but a fancy job title born of nepotism and access to a movie star. Each year, I stared down a pile of unpalatable scripts and sadly resigned myself to spending the better part of my waking hours reading them. But all of these things only contributed to a slow build of ennui that, sadly, I could live with; nothing really jarred me into quitting. Not until a project I actually cared about got made.

'Gesine, what are you doing here? I'd never have noticed if you didn't come.'

That's what did it. That's why I quit, that one dickish, dismissive greeting. It didn't even make sense. But what it was was mean. And it was uttered by a man I'd spent months helping get to this very place, the party to celebrate the start of his project. A project that for months no one wanted. And the damn party I'd helped plan, for God's sake.

I'd set up meeting after meeting with studios, shilled the idea to anyone who would listen, helped organise showcases, filled the seats with high-powered suits, and then finally, in a last-ditch effort, my Hollywood Hail Mary, made a grovelling call to a friend in a very high place begging for an introduction to the one person who could make it happen. And that one call led to a fortuitous creative confluence that resulted in a 'go' project. And now that this guy had a career and a soon-to-be household name, he thought it was okay to treat one of the little people who did the idiot grunt work like a subhuman. So what was I doing there?

A day later, still smarting from that comment, I was in my car on a studio lot muttering to myself like a crazy woman. I stopped long enough to call Ray.

'I've had it. I want out of this douchebaggery.'

I do care about cake. There really aren't any new ideas in baking; it's the same confectionary plot again and again, perhaps in different combinations. But everything I bake is a story worth retelling. Working through lunch, the air thick with almonds and chocolate, I tend to the elements of my layer cakes, the acts that make up the whole, never losing sight of what they will become but taking joy in the deliciousness of each individual part. Buttercream, ganache, almond cake, marzipan; layering each element in perfect symmetry, so when I slice the long cake into individual pieces with a scalding hot knife, each layer is distinct and uniform. I carefully transfer the slices to the pastry tray and put any stray bits of cake on a plate for the crew to nibble, evidence of a lunchtime well spent.

Opera Cake

OPERA CAKE IS TRADITIONALLY made with layers of almond sponge cake. In its natural state, almond sponge is, yes, spongy, but also a bit dry. Common practice is to soak the sponge with simple syrup; in this application, simple syrup laced with strong coffee.

I think this is utter horseshit. Why not use a moist almond cake to start? Usually the saving grace of opera slices is the filling and the thin layer of almond paste that covers the very top of the cake. But the layers of sponge cake are very thin and with the soaked-cake approach, they become so sodden with simple syrup that there's no possibility of peeling them off efficiently enough to just get down and dirty with the good stuff, the filling.

I use an almond cake that puts sponge to shame. I use a scale to measure out the ingredients for perfection. It's easy to get this one wrong with shoddy measuring.

When there are stray bits, I stack the errant pieces on a plate and set them on the workstation by the door leading from the bakery to the front of the house. It's for this cake that my crew pays me the highest compliment: 'I hate you. I hate you for doing this to me. You are an evil woman.' And within seconds, it disappears.

SERVES 8

For the almond cake
Nonstick cooking spray

1½ packages (each package is usually around 7 ounces) or 10 ounces almond paste, broken into small bits

1 cup sugar

2 ounces (¼ cup) honey

½ pound (2 sticks) unsalted butter, at room temperature

6 large eggs

⅞ cup all-purpose flour

½ teaspoon baking powder

½ teaspoon salt

For the chocolate ganache
1 cup heavy cream

2 tablespoons sugar

2 tablespoons corn syrup

4 tablespoons (½ stick) unsalted butter

1 pound semisweet chocolate, finely chopped

For the mocha buttercream

10 egg whites

¼ cup brewed coffee with 1 tablespoon instant
espresso dissolved in the coffee, cooled

2 cups sugar

1 pound (4 sticks) unsalted butter, at room
temperature, cut into 1-inch cubes

1 cup chocolate ganache

FOR THE MARZIPAN LAYER

One 7-ounce package almond paste, rolled out into a thin layer onto a large piece of parchment so that it's the same size as the top of the finished cake. Cover the almond layer with another piece of parchment to keep from drying out and set aside.

FOR THE ALMOND CAKE

Preheat the oven to 325°F/170°C. Liberally spray a ½ sheet pan (18 x 13 inches) with nonstick cooking spray and line it with parchment paper.

In the bowl of an electric mixer fitted with the whisk attachment, combine the remaining almond paste, sugar, and honey. Beat until well combined. Scrape the sides of the bowl now and again to make sure no bits of almond paste are left behind. If you don't whip the mixture well enough, stray chunks of almond paste will make the batter lumpy.

Add the butter in small bits, scraping the bowl down at least twice in the process.

Add the eggs one by one, beating until each is completely incorporated. After each addition, scrape down the sides of the bowl. After the last egg, beat on high until the batter is fluffy.

On the lowest speed, slowly incorporate the flour, baking powder, and salt until blended.

Spread the batter evenly in the prepared pan. Bake until the cake is golden brown and springs back when you touch it, 15 to 20 minutes. Let cool completely.

FOR THE CHOCOLATE GANACHE

In a saucepan, bring the cream, sugar, corn syrup, and butter to a boil over moderate heat, whisking until the sugar is dissolved.

Remove from heat and add the chocolate, whisking until smooth.

Allow the ganache to cool, stirring occasionally, until spreadable. If the ganache cools so much that it is impossible to spread, transfer it to a microwavable container and nuke for 30 seconds at a time, stirring after each 30 seconds.

FOR THE MOCHA BUTTERCREAM

Combine the egg whites, coffee, and sugar in the bowl of an electric mixer. Place over a saucepan of simmering water and whisk until the sugar is dissolved and the mixture reaches 160°F/70°C (high enough to kill the bad stuff). Whisk vigorously and constantly; you don't want scrambled eggs. You can dip your finger into the egg whites and rub them together to make sure the sugar has dissolved.

Transfer the bowl to a mixer fitted with the whisk attachment and whisk on high until the egg whites have tripled in size and are cool and shiny (about 10 minutes).

With the mixer on low, start dropping cubes of butter into the egg whites; then return to high until the buttercream thickens and is spreadable. On low, add the cup of ganache. Mix until completely incorporated.

TO ASSEMBLE THE CAKE

Cut the almond cake lengthwise into three even strips. Use a ruler; don't eyeball it.

Spread 1 cup of buttercream onto the first layer. Transfer to the refrigerator until the buttercream is set but not hard, about 15 minutes.

Carefully place a second layer of almond cake on top of the buttercream. Make sure the cake is level.

Spread 1 cup of ganache over the second layer, making sure that everything is level. Take your time with each layer to ensure evenness. Return to the refrigerator until just set, another 15 minutes.

Place the third layer of cake on top of the ganache and spread ¼ to ½ a cup of buttercream in a very thin layer over the top. Keeping the almond paste on the parchment, carefully transfer the thin layer to the cake and invert it over the cake so that it completely covers the top layer, trimming any part that hangs over with scissors or a sharp knife.

Spread a thin layer of ganache over the almond paste and return to the refrigerator for at least an hour.

Using a ruler, mark guidelines in the ganache every 3 inches. With a hot, dry knife, carefully cut even slices. Transfer each slice to a platter or individual plate with a large offset spatula or a pie spatula for balance as you cut it.

Make sure the filling is very cool and firm and that your knife is damn hot and very dry. Otherwise, the slices will be messy. You don't want messy slices. It's hard to bring yourself to eat this cake when you get it right; it's such a lovely little layered thing and it took a lot of patience to get it perfect. But it's as tasty as it is beautiful. So admire it but please eat it.

Chapter Twelve

Tiers of Frustration

12 p.m.

THE SECOND MY MORNING DUTIES END, my mind turns to my big baking projects of the week: two anniversaries, a baby shower, and a thirtieth-birthday cake. And then there are the commitment ceremonies and weddings. They're not only big, they're a big pain in the ass.

Wedding cakes are as much engineering feats as they are pastry. The bigger they get, the more architectural support they need. Each individual tier has to be exact, perfectly plumb, before you can stack the next. Many bakers make nothing but wedding cakes. Some bakers refuse to make them at all. The stress that accompanies making a single wedding cake occupies weeks of a baker's life.

I once read an article entitled 'Tips for Your Budget Wedding' wherein the wedding 'expert' insisted that brides-to-be shouldn't tell the baker they're ordering a wedding cake. Instead, they should just say it's for a large party, because bakers inflate the prices for wedding cakes.

Excuse me? This may jive for the poseur who keeps a fake tiered cake in the backroom and shoves a Duncan Hines cupcake on top so there's something to slice into, while the caterers serve up Crisco-infused blobs from a nasty sheet cake for the guests. But it won't fly for the baker who painstakingly bakes and assembles each tier, delivers them in pieces, and then builds the real deal on location. If someone lied to me and told me the day before the event that the cake I was making was now a tiered colossus that I'd have to deliver and assemble on-site, I'd tell them to screw themselves and get a Carvel Cookiepuss.

But for all the *agita* that comes with making a wedding cake, like the paranoid bride with the LL Bean tote bag full of tearsheets from *Martha Stewart Weddings*, or an ingredient nitpicking mother of the bride with a deadly peanut allergy, nothing can rattle me after the disaster that was my very first wedding cake.

The summer of 2005 our shop was finished, with all the bells and whistles. But we couldn't have our grand opening until my sister got married in late July because

I was making her four-tiered wedding cake. And I'd never tiered anything in my life, certainly not cake.

I blacked out the months before on the calendar and did nothing but make practice wedding cakes. I stacked tiers, piped beaded borders, and then asked random strangers who passed by our shuttered shop if they by chance were in need of a wedding cake on the fly. I just happened to have a few extra sitting around.

We flew to LA a week before the big day. I had a master schedule planned out. I'd bake the layers for the large cake and groom's cake, fill them with buttercream, give them a smooth topcoat, and let them firm up in the fridge. The actually assembly, stacking the tiers and decorative piping, would take place on-site. That was day one. Then I'd move on to the two hundred individual cakes Sandy wanted for all the guests. The big cake was for cutting and general plunder. The individual cakes were for dessert. That was day two. The third day I would devote to the wedding favours: little bags containing five different-flavoured macaroons each. The rest of the week was for final touches. And on the day before the big day, we'd drive the two hours to the wedding site, where I'd assemble the cake right away. This would give me the morning of the wedding to decorate myself for maid-of-honour duties.

When we got to my sister's house, Ray put away our bags and I cranked up the oven. Not a peep, and it was on full convection mode. I thought, 'That's what you get when you can pay out the nose for quality.' The fan was pumping away inside, but you'd never know it. 'Hmmm, maybe it's too quiet.' I opened the oven door. The fan wasn't moving. It wasn't getting warm. I tried turning it on again. Nothing.

I called every repair company in the phone book and no one was available. Not until midweek.

I stared at the ovens for two days. When the repairman showed up, I was wild-eyed and waiting with pans filled with cake batter. I had one day. One freakin' day to do everything.

The morning we had to leave, Ray got the van ready. We loaded the cakes into the back, leaving the van running and the air conditioning blasting while we ran back inside to get our luggage. We had to be quick about it. The van was on the street and outside the security zone of the garage. And the paparazzi were lurking about the neighbourhood. We couldn't have them follow us to the wedding site.

When we got back, the van was locked. The keys were inside the van, the cakes were inside the van, but we weren't.

We called AAA and waited. The sun was barely out and it was already dripping hot outside. But the cakes looked cool and collected, hanging out in the idling air-conditioned box.

Once we were rescued, we noticed a tidy queue of

SUVs full of paparazzi waiting for us to leave so they could neatly pursue. We delicately turned onto Sunset Boulevard with a block-long vehicular escort. And as we approached the onramp to the highway, the van careened off toward the emergency lane, the back tire 'THWAP THWAP THWAPing' and throwing off shredded bits into traffic as we rolled to a stop. We lost the paparazzi but we lost precious time as well.

At the wedding site, our little refrigerated van sat alone overnight in a field. I got there first thing on the wedding day to find it still waiting in the white-hot sunshine and 100-degree heat. We borrowed a table from catering who'd taken up the entirety of the kitchen and left no space for me. We set up a makeshift workstation inside the car. A young woman from catering was assigned to be my helper, and we got to work in the tiny walk-in fridge on wheels.

Seven hours later and I still wasn't done. The ceremony was in an hour. My hands were shaking and I was scared to ask whether the cake was really drifting off to one side or was I just loopy from leaning over a three-foot tall cake with a pastry bag and piping beads of frosting the size of poppy seeds along the edges. I was working in romantic mood lighting, the dome light on the ceiling of the cabin revealing just enough for me to make out the general outline of the cake. Every few minutes, I'd kick open the door and let the natural light crash in to get a better look. That's when I noticed that the cake was lopsided.

When Ray came to check on me, I stared at him for a minute, my sticky hands wrapped tightly around a piping bag oozing melting buttercream from multiple tears in the plastic. The minute I figured out the right angle to avoid squirting frosting from an errant hole in the bag, I'd spring a new leak. My tank top was taking one for the team; all the extra icing found a home in the cotton ridges. A little found its way into my hair.

'Time's up.'

So there it was. The cake had to be finished now and I had a half hour to look presentable. I wrapped my globby paws around the trick pastry bag and planted my feet resolutely.

'Fuck it. I'll just hide the ugly bits with flowers.'

Coiffed, scrubbed of stray bits of frosting, and zipped into my dress, I made a break for the catering tent and found my cake. Sitting upright. A florist gently placing fresh flowers along the bottom edge turned to me, not knowing I was the baker, and gestured to the cake.

'Isn't it beautiful?'

'Yeah. Yeah, it really is.' God I was relieved, but I just had to ask, 'Does it seem, though, that it may be leaning just a little to the right?'

This Saturday, I have no bridesmaid's duties to attend to, no paparazzi to outrun. But I feel the same amount of obligation, the same desire to create the perfect dream for this stranger bride as I did years ago for my sister. But please, God, go a little easy on the theatrics this time.

Carrot Cake

RAY CALLED ME AT WORK in LA on our friend Jeff's birthday. Jeff's wife, Terri, was having a hard time finding a decent carrot cake in town, and would I have any ideas? I gathered my things and ran straight to the grocery store to get supplies. Hell, no one needed to ask twice. I was born for this.

I had a few hours before the party started. I jury-rigged a recipe I thought would be solid and worked around it to make sure that the cake would be moist and flavourful and the cream cheese frosting tangy, sweet, and abundant. It looked like hell, though. I had to frost it warm. Never frost a cake when the layers are warm. Never. But everyone who ate it fell deeply in lust.

The next time I made it, the cake was for my sister. And she too fell madly in love. So it came to be that this simple little cake became a very grand wedding cake. Now it can be yours to make for any and all occasions.

For the cake

1½ cups vegetable oil, plus additional for the pans

2 cups sugar

4 large eggs

2 cups all-purpose flour

2 teaspoons baking powder

2 teaspoons baking soda

1 teaspoon salt

1 teaspoon cinnamon

¾ teaspoon nutmeg

3 cups finely grated peeled carrots (about 1 pound)

For the frosting

4 cups confectioners' sugar

Two 8-ounce packages cream cheese, at room
    temperature

8 tablespoons (1 stick) unsalted butter, at room
    temperature

1 teaspoon vanilla extract

FOR THE CAKE

Preheat the oven to 325°F/170°C. Lightly grease
three 8-inch round cake pans with 1½-inch sides.

Line the bottoms of the pans with wax paper and lightly grease the paper.

Place the sugar and oil in the bowl of an electric mixer and beat until combined. Add the eggs one at a time, beating well after each addition.

Sift the flour, baking powder, baking soda, salt, cinnamon, and nutmeg into the sugar and oil mixture and beat on low until all ingredients are incorporated. Stir in the carrots.

Pour the batter into the prepared pans, dividing equally. Bake about 45 minutes, until a toothpick inserted into the centre comes out clean, if you must. But you can also gently press the top; if it springs back and if the cake begins to pull away from the sides of the pan, it's done. Set the cakes on racks and let them cool in the pans 15 minutes. Invert the cakes onto the racks and cool completely. (Cakes can be made 1 day ahead. Wrap tightly in plastic and store at room temperature.)

FOR THE FROSTING

In an electric mixer, beat all the ingredients with the whisk attachment until smooth and creamy.

TO ASSEMBLE THE CAKE

Place one completely cool cake layer on a lovely cake platter. Spread with ¾ cup frosting.

Top with another cake layer. Spread with ¾ cup frosting.

Top with the remaining cake layer. Using an offset spatula, spread the remaining frosting in decorative swirls over the sides and top of the cake.

Chapter Thirteen

A Grand Opening

1 p.m.

M Y WORKSTATION FACES a one-way mirror, so I have a hazy view of the store at all times. It was a great idea. By putting in a police-grade interrogation mirror, I'd theoretically have a clear view of the front of the house but could keep my painfully shy self hidden in the back where I could work fearlessly, unseen by prying eyes. In practice, the results weren't as stellar as I'd hoped. Watch any cop show and you'll know perfectly well that the perp sits in a well-lit room, sweating just a bit, as he's grilled by Detective #1. Detective #2 is standing in the dark in the adjoining room, watching the whole scene from the viewing side of the one-way mirror. The operative phrase being 'in the dark.' I can't bake in the dark. My ceiling is atwitter with rows of fluorescents. So the general effect is of watching shadow puppets through gauze. From inside the store, looking at the mirror side of the glass, you do see a decent reflection. But if the lighting is just right and you squint, a smidgen of the behind-the-scenes proceedings is unveiled.

I spent most of our grand opening day avoiding looking through that glass.

It was only 1 p.m. and Little Cool Whip, my makeshift baking apprentice, was having issues with the 96-degree heat and was losing her pants, exposing her alarmingly bony white hips and butterfly tattoo. She got her nickname early on when she revealed that she didn't care for real whipped cream or fresh-baked anything. She favoured the packaged, artificial stuff and wasn't about to change her ways. So we called her Cool Whip and somehow she was fine with that. A conveyor belt of sweat propelled her glasses perilously close to the edge of her nose and, spellbound, I waited to see if she could save them before they slipped into her cake batter. We were sharing a fan, switching stations every ten minutes to get full-frontal air circulation.

Henry, our heating and cooling guy, assured me that air conditioning wasn't customary in local bakeries because it doesn't get hot here. But as I watched a side of buttercream slide off the side of my cake like a piece of Alaskan glacial shelf succumbing to global warming, I got the sneaking suspicion that he didn't know what the hell he was talking about.

Cool Whip, of the concave clavicle, was the only hire we'd made. It was a small store and we had small ambitions. We figured we'd get a few customers in our first few weeks and grow by word of mouth. This way, we'd be able to learn on the job at a comfortable pace. So she was our part-timer, working with me from 5 a.m. to early afternoon and then leaving for her shift as a line cook at Vermont's busiest roadside diner, the Wayside.

Out front, Sandy and Ray worked like pros, Ray making espresso drinks and Sandy manning the register and packing up pastries. She tied up each box with a flourish. It had occurred to us, the night before, that Ray might have too much on his hands with both the register and the espresso machine on our first day, even though we hadn't advertised our opening. So my sister took a few hours to memorise the register and offered her services as counter lady in exchange for unlimited coffee and pastries. We'd spent a week together stocking shelves and prepping. It was officially her honeymoon, but Sandy wouldn't be anywhere else. Manning the register seemed easy and safe enough.

By late morning we had a line that stretched out the front door and continued down the block. Vermont may be rural, but its residents can text as fast as anyone in the big city. And everyone who walked in the door IM'd ten friends to tell them there was a movie star serving pastries on Elm Street.

Our local news crew knocked on the kitchen door to ask for an interview. I wasn't in any condition and I didn't have the time. So the news team set up sticks across the street and started interviewing the poor souls waiting in line in sweltering heat. Sandy poked her head into the kitchen every few minutes.

'Associated Press is here, they'd like a few words.'

'Your local news anchor is here, she wants an exclusive.'

'The governor's here. He'd like to pop in and say hello.'

And so it went, for the entire day. A line of local dignitaries to the left, waiting to catch sight of the movie star under the guise of wanting to speak with me. And then a line to the right composed of local civilians waiting to catch sight of the movie star under the guise that they wanted pastry. We were wiped out of everything. No cakes or cookies. We'd ground the last bag of coffee beans. Our shelves were bare. We had to start this all over at 4 a.m. in the morning, but we still had to wash a mountain of dishes and clean the kitchen and the store. We put the closed sign up an hour early. We called in for pizza, our friends Whit and Caroline drove in an hour from town to wash dishes, and we locked up at 10 p.m. When we got home, we turned on the local news. We were the headline story.

Ray called Jenny, who lived in the neighbourhood, happened to be a trained barista, and had offered her help when she saw what we were up against on our opening day. So for the next few days Sandy hung out in the back, washing dishes, organising, helping me bake, and answering phones with a very strange accent. When she had a moment to sit, she dragged a chair from the office and sat next to me with the laptop and started going through our shop emails.

'Your inbox says 8,000.'

'What do you mean? What does 8,000 mean?'

'It means you have 8,000 new emails. Should I look at them?'

Every email, each one, was an order for macaroons. And the number kept going up every time we hit the Refresh button. The news of our minuscule shop opening had spread a little farther than rural Vermont. The Associated Press news service carried the story to every small-town outlet in America; it was in *USA Today* and on the national evening news. An AP photographer had made his way into the shop. He agreed to take pictures of pastries only, nothing and no one else. He lied. A picture of Sandy mid-pastry transaction was splashed over the international newswire and was voted *Newsweek* readers' favourite picture of the week. While this would have been a boon to a mass-production facility manned by Keebler elves, it was a catastrophic scenario for a fledgling bakery manned by a lone pastry chef and a paper-thin part-time assistant. The workload involved in keeping the shop filled was breaking me. The added weight of Internet orders threatened to shut us down on the first day.

Our crew started to expand. Cool Whip quit her diner job and came on full time. On our day off, I hired part-time workers to scoop macaroon dough to fulfil orders. We hired a dishwasher and more kitchen crew. Our neighbour Joanne volunteered her time and assembled hundreds of shipping boxes in our tiny back office; we had to dig her out of her cardboard dungeon at the end of each day. And Ray kept his eyes open for counter help. He'd never intended on making this his full-time job. But it was starting to look like one.

Sandy had to leave eventually and when she did, Ray and I were really and truly on our own. She made one last circuit of the kitchen with a label maker, adhering little inventory tags to shelves and drawers to keep them organised. She dipped into the sink and finished off the dishes, her manicure ruined by now and the tender flesh around her nail beds waterlogged.

Today I look through the glass to the outside world in the shop pretty fearlessly. We still get lines out the door midmorning when regulars are joncsing for breakfast and a shot of caffeine. But there's a trained staff, not a movie star among them, who handle transactions and barista duties with aplomb. I've got a trim staff in back, but we're efficient and can keep up with demand.

There's a picture of me on our grand opening morning from our local paper, grinning the manic grin of a sleep-deprived idiot who had no business opening a pastry shop. It was the hottest August on record and I'd taken to wearing colourful kerchiefs on my head, believing this was an attractive way to keep my hair back. My face was gloriously sweaty and my apron encrusted with flour and chocolate. Now it's three years later and we've survived. Just barely.

We finally have air conditioning. And I've got a lovely collection of kerchiefs in the back if you are interested.

Apple Pie

ON OPENING DAY, I had a rather limited selection. Small carrot cakes, chocolate cakes, fruit tarts, croissants, scones, and sticky buns.

Toward late morning, I brought out little apples pies and within minutes they were gone. My apple pie is damn good. So good, in fact, that I had to make a decision. Either make pie every day and drive myself crazy with the work hours that go into it, or limit pies to a single day of the week. I took the second option, and now Friday is pie day. You're guaranteed to see caramel apple pies, small and large, in all their glory. Along with cherry, blueberry, lemon meringue, banana cream, and coconut cream.

For any pie, the crust is king. Most American piecrust recipes call for lard or shortening to get that typical diner-dough tenderness. I can't get on board with that; I like a little flakiness too. And that means pounds of butter. So I go straight for the mother lode, quick puff pastry.

As for the apples, I caramelise them first. Cooking them a bit in advance, along with butter, sugar, and a few spices, gives the filling a complex and mouthwatering flavour. It also fixes the problem of filling your pie high with raw apples, covering them with your second layer of dough, and then finding that while the top crust is still appealingly lofty, all the apples have baked away to nothing inside. By caramelising the apples first, you're guaranteed that the contents won't settle during baking; when you cut into a tall pie, you'll find tall layers of apples.

MAKES ONE DOUBLE CRUSTED PIE

For quick puff pastry
4 cups all-purpose flour
1¼ pounds (5 sticks) cold unsalted butter
1 teaspoon salt
¼ teaspoon lemon juice stirred into ¾ cup cold
    water

For the filling
8 Granny Smith apples
Juice of 1 lemon
½ cup packed light brown sugar
½ cup granulated sugar
¼ cup all-purpose flour
1 teaspoon cinnamon

¼ teaspoon nutmeg

¼ teaspoon cloves

½ teaspoon salt

4 tablespoons (½ stick) unsalted butter

1 teaspoon vanilla extract

¼ cup heavy cream

1 large egg

Sanding sugar

FOR THE PUFF PASTRY

Place the flour in a large bowl. Cut the butter into 1-inch pieces. Add to the flour and incorporate with your hands, pinching and massaging the butter into the flour, making sure to leave discernible chunks of butter intact. You don't want to incorporate the butter so well that it is starts to look like cornmeal. Chunks of butter are good.

Dissolve the salt in the water. Add to the flour and butter and mix gently with your hands until dough comes together slightly.

Shape the dough into a rough square and let it rest for 10 minutes.

On a lightly floured surface, roll the dough into a ½-inch-thick rectangle. Give the dough three single turns, followed by one double turn. If the dough feels rubbery after you have completed a few turns, let it rest a few minutes before you continue. Cover and refrigerate. Your dough block should be approximately 12 x 6 inches.

FOR THE FILLING

Peel and slice the apples. Sprinkle with lemon juice. Combine the sugars, flour, cinnamon, nutmeg, cloves, and salt in a large bowl, add the apples, and toss to coat.

In a sturdy pot large enough to hold the apples, melt the butter with the vanilla and cream. Add the apples and cook until the fruit is soft and the mixture thickens.

TO ASSEMBLE THE PIE

Once your quick puff is nice and cool, take a sharp knife and cut in half. Take a look at the dough where you've sliced through. You should see layers of dough and butter. Some larger chunks of butter will be peeking through. This is a wonderful thing. When you roll, you want to press down on these layers. You don't want to lay the cut side down; make sure the layers are parallel to the rolling table and you are pressing the layers down into each other, maintaining the layer structure and ensuring maximum puff and flakiness. Roll each piece into a 10-inch circle. Transfer the first circle to a pie plate and crimp the edges. Freeze for at least ½ hour. Wrap the second 10-inch round in plastic and refrigerate until you are ready to assemble the pie.

When you are ready to bake, preheat the oven to 350°F/180°C. Take the frozen pie shell from the freezer and with a fork, stab the bottom of the shell a few times. Line the shell with foil or parchment and fill it with dry beans or rice as a weight. Bake until the edges are slightly golden and the bottom of the shell no longer looks wet and raw, about 15 minutes. This is called blind baking and ensures that the bottom pastry won't be soggy.

Beat the egg with 1 tablespoon water to make an egg wash.

Remove the foil and the rice or beans and transfer the filling to the shell. Place your second dough circle on top of the apples. Brush the top of the dough with the egg wash and sprinkle with sanding sugar. Bake at 350°F/180°C until the top crust is golden brown and the filling is bubbling, about 45 minutes.

At this point, you may be upset that the pie doesn't have that perfect edge that most double-crust pies have. There's a very good reason: usually great-looking pies are composed of crappy pastry that doesn't puff and flake. The dough is bland

and hard and pretty much comes out of the oven looking exactly like it did in its unbaked form. But these pies also don't benefit from the initial blind bake; instead the filling is added to the unbaked bottom layer of pastry, the second pastry disk is placed on top, and the edges of the bottom and top crusts are crimped together. It keeps everything so tidy! But who wants a perfect-looking pie with a dry, hard crust and a soggy bottom?

Chapter Fourteen

Lamb of God and Star Giant

2 p.m.

THERE'S A LULL IN THE STORE between 2 and 3 p.m. Lunch service is all but over; everyone in town is back at work digesting. We're puttering away in the back, prepping for the morning. In the front of the house, there's a little organisation and cleaning going on. Our afternoon pastry and coffee pushers, Meeka and Phayvahn, are organising the shelves. I look after them from the kitchen, the mother hen. I never thought I had a maternal side.

I blame Agnes and Adrienne for finding it. They were the rambunctious kids manning the counter in our early days. The moment the lull hit, they'd start searching for the store football. They'd bolt outside, leaving the store unmanned, and start a ribald and perilous game of touch football in the middle of the street, drafting unsuspecting joggers onto their teams and dive-bombing passing cars with their loopy passes, stopping oncoming traffic and chasing the pigskin as it headed straight for the storm drain.

On Fridays, we celebrate pie day and fill the store top to tail with any and all manner of pies. But for Agnes and Adrienne, it was also 'lie day,' and they would spin outlandish yarns for unsuspecting customers. Agnes had half of the town convinced that she was a grandmother twice over at the age of twenty-five.

We came by Agnes and Adrienne through Jenny. Jenny lived in the Meadow, around the corner from where we were tearing apart and putting together our little shop. During construction we had an open door policy with the neighbourhood and let the curious peek in and check out the progress. Jenny would stop by and talk coffee with Ray. She was a self-proclaimed coffee geek, opinionated about coffee, its preparation, and the people who made it and drank it. A tiny woman, she had jet-black pixie hair, huge knockers, and a colourful profanity-laden vocabulary. A high school dropout but a coffee scholar and barista by trade and obsession, she had a keen interest in our opening. She'd been trying to open a shop of her own, so we were potential competition. Everyone else in the neighbourhood who stopped in said the same thing: 'Oh, man. I've always wanted a store like this in Montpelier. Too bad it won't do well.' Jenny never said this. She knew that success came with anything made beautifully.

She came to our opening. She stood in line for an hour and ordered an iced Americano from Ray and then gave him step-by-step instructions on how to make it. Then she asked if he needed help. She started the next day.

For Jenny and Ray, coffee was high art. They riffed on the machine like jazz musicians and pulled magic out of a pretty crap machine. But they were handling the busy load in the front of the house alone and getting on each other's nerves. We needed to start looking for more employees.

Bonnie was a regular. She got a latte every day and occasionally bought a devil's cream pie. She was a transplant from upmarket Newport, Rhode Island, and every so often let slip a bit of Newport blueblood lockjaw into her banter. Sometimes she'd let out a resounding 'Holy fuck-oly'. The minute she started working the counter, she had every customer either eating from her palm or scared witless.

After Bonnie, Jenny brought us Agnes. Her first day of work, she came through the kitchen doors, gloriously Rubenesque and rosy-cheeked, and said, 'Today is the best day ever!'

I find that kind of unbridled optimism suspect.

So does Ray. We'd been knee-deep in plastic cheer in Hollywood; it was never sincere and usually hid something quite sinister.

Agnes's unflappable buoyancy and overall goodwill rankled Ray. He was having none of it. He suspected her of chicanery. I'd already fallen in love; by day three Agnes convinced me that she could make any day the best day ever. The girl made ice sculptures and was the only human who could drink me under the table. Every day she'd come in and ask me things like, 'Does a cow "moo" in German? And does a dog "woof"? If not, what on earth do they say?' Her name means lamb of God, for God's sake. I even let her hug me.

For Ray, it took exactly two weeks. I peeked out the window to the shop and found Ray and Agnes involved in what looked like a fit of calisthenics. For a split second, I worried that Ray had broken a dam of rage burning inside dear Agnes. I wouldn't blame her if she was attacking him. I ran out to break it up.

They were in tears, laughing. Agnes figured that all Ray needed was a good bout of 'Head, Shoulders, Knees, and Toes,' a little exercise in which you sing along as you touch your head, shoulders, knees, and toes. They were bobbing up and down, gleeful idiots, in the middle of the store. She broke him from his disbelief. Who knew that someone so lovely existed? We didn't until we met Agnes.

And then came Adrienne. Pretty, blond, and achingly

funny, she's the girl that every insecure kid hates. She's also outrageously dyslexic. She'd want to be a movie star, if only she didn't have to work at it. So she'll settle for being generally fabulous. We started off calling her Star Child because of her unnatural fixation with the goings-on of young Hollywood, but she misheard it as Star Giant, which we all liked a hell of a lot better. So now that's her name. If the girls come in to visit with Ray, the boys all come to see Adrienne. She's lovely and kind and every once in a while she's feisty. She once told Larry, everyone's favourite customer, 'Larry, if only you were fifty years younger I'd marry you.'

There were the Sands Sisters. I had always been under the general impression that a child both home schooled and religious is dangerous, at the very least, and certainly humourless and easily offended – until I met Kalika and Meeka, the Sands Sisters. They have older siblings, all of them with relatively run-of-the-mill first names like Stephen and Erika. But a fit of genius struck Mr. and Mrs. Sands, and they gave their two youngest children, two young women who could easily have emerged from the Regency pages of Jane Austen, names befitting young women of character.

It took a while to figure them out. Kalika – tiny, sandy blond, with delicate features and crisp speech – started working with us first. Then Meeka joined us, bright blond, tall, and doe-eyed. They both lived at home, Kalika having just graduated from college and

Meeka still in college. They couldn't work Sundays – they went to church. I worried incessantly that they'd walk in the back during one of my many linguistic blue streaks and, deeply and morally offended, quit on the spot.

But they never spoke out against my rampant profanity. And Kalika, during an innocent conversation, described a recent night out at a local music spot as a 'veritable shit show'. She is always five minutes early to work. Meeka revealed an uncanny ability to find four-leaf clovers and is learning to play the harp. Ray and I decided that home schooling and religious dedication might actually be the only way to raise a child. These two had come out so well.

Then Mr. Sands was diagnosed with pancreatic cancer. It was, they knew, a death sentence for their father. But they also knew there were miracles. They kept showing up for work on time and in good cheer. Kalika mentioned that St. Anthony was a particular favourite of her father's. So in the morning, in the quiet time in the bathtub when the world was asleep, I prayed to St. Anthony. I prayed for a miracle for a kind man who had raised unbelievably lovely children. Even though I was buck naked among the bath bubbles and each time I said St. Anthony I felt compelled to say his name like a Jersey gangster, 'Ant-Knee,' I was still praying. And I was praying like I meant it. That's how good the Sands Sisters were.

But sometimes employees just don't work out. There was the kid whose daily habit of eating multiple bulbs of raw garlic in order to purge himself of the toxins of the world left everyone around him gasping for fresh air. Garlic is a little like skunk; you smell a hint of it far away and there's something strangely pleasant about it. Up close and personal, it's downright noxious.

There was the middle-aged woman who started off as the dream help we were desperate for, until she became increasingly unstable. She started to look at our young dishwasher like a ravenous wolf and, unsurprisingly, was making him feel very uncomfortable. We found out that not only was she generally emotionally erratic, she was also a convicted felony sex offender. We could have saved ourselves a lot of pain had we Googled the scamp.

So now we've taken to doing a quick search of prospective employees. Just in case. Young people, they're prone to drunken hijinks, and lately everyone is documenting their youthful indiscretions and posting the evidence online. I've got no problem with that. I once did a backbend in the middle of a local watering hole at college after a sloppy date with Mr. Bacardi. I was hosting a little shindig called 'Jamnesty' to raise money for Amnesty International and to get signatures on petitions in hopes of securing the release of poor souls trapped in foreign prisons for speaking their minds. Or maybe for posting drunken pictures of themselves. A local made me an offer: 'Girl, I'll sign that thing if you do a backbend over that rope.' It was a red rope dividing the bar area from the dance floor. I'm a dedicated human rights activist. And I was very drunk. Problem is I'm not limber. So once I got myself into the backbend, I couldn't get out of it. I wish I had a picture of that moment because I've never been able to do a backbend since.

Long story longer than it needed to be, the bottom line is that I understand, and I expect to find embarrassing pictures of prospective employees online. What I don't expect is to find a close-up of a prospective employee's lady parts. Posted not by some evil ex-boyfriend who took the pictures unbeknownst to the poor girl, but by the proud owner of the coochie herself. On a popular public forum. Multiple pictures. And once the pictures loaded, I said what any slightly open minded but really kind of prudish woman would say: 'Oh, for f*ck's sake.'

By all means, be proud of your nether blossom. Take pictures if you like. But I've got to wonder about your judgment if you plaster them like billboards on the information superhighway. I'm sure you'd say that if you were working in my establishment, you'd keep your bits under wraps. But how can I be positive? And what if I find you posting a picture of one of my pastries in a compromising position? I don't think I can live with that.

Then there are the dishwashers, and even with a thorough Google search, we get some prizewinners. When we finally finagle someone into taking up the challenge, they end up either landing in jail, going back into rehab, or heading straight to the hospital on their own time, despite my suspicions that dishwashing here at Gesine's drove them there. Of our never-ending string of dishwashers, the first went to jail; the second drove herself crazy from the monotony and started to rock back and forth, humming maniacally as she scrubbed. Then she ran away to the circus. Our third, Matt, was showing some emotional fortitude, so I promoted him right out of dishwashing to retain his sanity and help in the baking. He was also skinny enough to fit into the ovens and liked curling up inside when they were off to scrub them clean. You can't lose that kind of talent, unless they're also aspiring musicians. Then they'll leave you in search of rock-and-roll stardom like Matt did. He didn't buy it when I told him that chicks dig bakers as much as sensitive singer-songwriters.

Our fourth dishwasher would leave for costume changes, returning in sequins or clown wigs. Whatever struck her fancy. The fifth I adored because she had such a bubbly attitude, but it turned out she was always funny and happy because she was always drunk. The sixth was the girl who worked for three days and scrubbed everything like a demon, but didn't show up on the fourth. Her boyfriend came to the store 'sweating in a manner inappropriate to the day,' as Bonnie described him, and told no one in particular that his girlfriend was in the hospital from drinking too much punch. Our dishwasher later told us that she had no idea the stuff was laced, to which the rest of us replied, 'Any party punch is laced unless you're in elementary school.' And then there was the unfortunate girl who started her shift by licking the stacked bowls clean, stole the last chocolate chip cookie from the still-warm sheet pan, snuck into the cooler, grabbed a handful of sliced brie and another fistful of bacon, and then locked herself in the bathroom for hours.

Our current dishwasher Nancy drags herself in in the morning just at that critical moment when we're about to open but haven't gotten everything out yet. The faint smell of Parliament menthols clings to her wife beater. Her utter lack of perceptible consciousness, so contrary to the manic panic we're whipping up, always manages to piss me off. I want her to walk in and acknowledge our stress, to lock into our lunatic energy and get crazy on the dirty dishes. But she sidles up to the sinks and gives everything a lazy once-over. The heaps of dishes, in arrangements so architecturally dicey you'd think we'd piled them with malice, seem to strike her as a vague nuisance that she's not ready to fully embrace. She also has a very tenuous relationship with gravity, so the second she moves to organising the multitude, there are thunderclaps of crashing pots and shattering plates. We're not holding out much hope for Nancy. Her hands have begun to shake, she speaks to herself as she's rinsing off caked dough from mixing bowls, and her eyes are glazing over. I'm betting she's got less than a month before she falls off her recovery wagon and lands back in a court-appointed detox. Tim and I discuss whether or not we should call her outpatient rehab facility and tell them our concerns. We live in a strange town, aptly nicknamed Montpeculiar, where any and all of her symptoms are embodied in most of our downtown residents and more than a few of our local politicians. So we're having a hard time telling whether she's just exhibiting the standard symptoms of being a local or whether she's in trouble.

I'd never managed more than a handful of employees. In Hollywood in the early 2000s, just four of us manned an entire entertainment company. And while I, along with my sister, was the boss, we were all productive adults who needed very little supervision, and that didn't much lend itself to developing a maternal affection.

But despite some odd ducks, every day Ray and I are amazed at how lucky we are with the people who end up staying. And invariably, the people we fall in love with and never want to leave, grow up a little at our shop and move on.

So when Agnes told us she was hanging up her espresso tamp for good, finishing college, and getting a big-girl job, I wept. When Adrienne made the announcement that she was moving to New York City, I fell into a deep depression. Then Jenny moved to another town and started up her own shop. And Cool Whip moved away to work at the Olive Garden. Everyone leaves with our blessing for their futures, but we curse them all the same for making us care about them, changing us in ways we were determined not to be changed, and then leaving us with an empty position to fill.

In the meantime, if you see a want ad in the paper that reads like this: 'Nice people wanted for work in pastry/coffee shop. We're as flexible as a gummi bear in the hot summer sun', you know that we're hiring. But be forewarned. If we like you, we may not let you go.

New England

THE NEW ENGLAND CAKE marries both the old and the new England and reminds me of the insane joviality and old school Vermontness of Agnes, Adrienne, and the Sands Sisters. The pound cake is a play on the very traditional and well-loved UK dessert staple, sticky toffee pudding. By adding the deep tones of coffee and brown sugar and the toffeelike bits of sweet dates, the cake takes on a very sophisticated flavour. Combine it with a Vermonty maple buttercream and the result is divine. The bright maple sweetness of the buttercream offsets the more earthy tones of the dense cake. This is a mature cake for mature audiences only. It's that sexy.

MAKES ONE 8-INCH THREE LAYER CAKE

For the cake

½ pound (2 sticks) unsalted butter, softened, plus additional for buttering the pan

3 cups sifted all-purpose flour, plus additional for dusting the pan

2 teaspoons baking powder

¾ teaspoon salt

3 cups packed light brown sugar

7 large eggs, at room temperature

2 teaspoons vanilla extract

½ cup heavy cream

½ cup hot coffee

1 cup chopped dates

For the buttercream

10 ounces egg whites (approximately 10 whites)

2 cups maple sugar (see Note)

1 pound (4 sticks) unsalted butter, at room
    temperature, cut into small pieces

Baker's Note: Maple sugar is most often a mail-order purchase but is sometimes available in health food stores. If you can't find it, use white sugar and add maple syrup to taste.

Preheat the oven to 350°F/180°C. Put the oven rack in the middle position.

For this recipe, you'll need three 8-inch cake pans. Generously butter the pans and dust with flour, knocking out the excess.

Sift the flour, baking powder, and salt into a bowl. Sift again into another bowl (the flour will have been sifted three times total).

Beat the butter and sugar in a large bowl with an electric mixer at medium-high speed until pale and fluffy, about 5 minutes in a stand mixer fitted with the paddle attachment or 6 to 8 minutes with a handheld mixer.

Add the eggs one at a time, beating well after each addition. Beat in the vanilla.

Reduce the speed to low and add half of the flour mixture, then all of the cream, then the remaining flour, mixing well after each addition. Scrape down the sides of bowl and add coffee and dates. Mix on low until evenly incorporated.

Spoon the batter into the prepared pans. Bake until the cake is golden and gently springs back when pressed, about 25 minutes.

Cool the cake in the pan on a rack for 30 minutes. Run a thin knife around the inner and outer edges, then set the rack over the pan and invert the cakes onto the rack to cool completely.

FOR THE BUTTERCREAM

Combine the egg whites and maple sugar in the bowl of an electric mixer set over a pan of simmering water. Whisk constantly until the sugar has completely melted and the mixture reaches

160°F/70°C. Transfer the bowl to the mixer and, using the whisk attachment, whisk on high until the meringue forms soft peaks. On low speed, add the butter slowly until completely incorporated. Beat again on high speed until the buttercream starts to thicken and become smooth.

TO ASSEMBLE THE CAKE

Spread 1 cup of buttercream on the first layer.

Stack the second layer on top and layer with another cup of buttercream.

Place the last layer on top and use the remaining buttercream to cover the top and sides of the cake.

Chapter Fifteen

The Sacred Time

3 p.m.

ANN AND ANNE COME IN AT 3 P.M. They order their coffees, get a few flourless chocolate hearts, and sit at the table by the front window and kibitz for about an hour. Mothers and daughters, friends, newly minted parents out for a stroll with their sleepy babies; at 3 p.m. there is a steady, gentle stream of easygoing pastry-hungry folks. This is when I miss my grandmother and my mother most.

For the German women of ritual who raised me – my mother and grandmother Omi – 3 p.m. was the best part of the day, the sacred time for cake and coffee. When we lived in Germany, I couldn't escape being roped into this ritual, and for a kid in the middle of high afternoon adventure, the timing was brutally off. Sitting still at that hour and savouring a hot beverage in a paper-thin porcelain cup was not a priority. And we didn't even get the good stuff. Coffee was reserved for the adults. The cake was a bonus, but being allowed to shove it into my face at high speed and be on my way would have made the moment sublime. Wasn't it enough to have to sit still without distraction through breakfast, lunch, and dinner with my family? Confining cake to the same ceremony was stupefying! When my mom took us back to the States, we continued our family meals but we were released from 3 p.m. cake and coffee; it was replaced by piano and ballet lessons and all the activities that fill an American kid's life.

My mother, sister, and I returned to Germany every few summers but I spent the entire summer of 1984, when I was fourteen, alone with Omi. She lived in a walk-up apartment across from a brewery in Nürnberg, the malodor of hot hops and yeast drenching the air. When Sandy and I had spent time there, we'd run up and down the six flights of stairs every few hours to the corner market. They sold Maoam chewy candies in packs of six individually wrapped morsels. Sandy's favourite was raspberry and mine was lemon, though I'd get an orange once in a while to remind me why I liked the lemon so much. We limited ourselves to a few each trip, convinced we'd control ourselves. At the end of a long rainy day in front of the TV watching unbearably amateurish German programming, we'd be buried under a mound of purple, yellow, and orange wrappers.

This time I flew by myself from Washington, D.C., to Frankfurt and took a connecting flight to Nürnberg, where Omi met me in her Fiat 500. It was scarcely bigger than my suitcase. We pushed the passenger seat as close to the dashboard as it would slide and muscled my bags into the back seat. Omi was so tiny her seat was already pushed forward to the same position. I crawled in and folded up my rangy legs, my shins pressed against the glove box and knees to my chin. Omi ignored the operational guide to the manual drive, as illustrated in the neat little drawing on the gearbox, opting to pass first and second entirely and pop straight into third, making my already compressed body feel as if it were passing into the supergravitational pull of a black hole. Once she hit the main thoroughfare, she gunned the car into fifth gear, hammered the gas pedal down with her bunioned foot, and set the car screaming, hell-bent for leather. As we crested a hill, she'd pop the gear into neutral and take us into a Niagara Falls barrel ride to the bottom. To her mind, this terror-filled nosedive was an economy of money and motion.

Omi maintained the same routine that I remembered from childhood: a small breakfast with tea; a large lunch of roasted potatoes, veal cutlet, butter lettuce salad, and a small bowl of sweetened yogurt with fresh fruit for dessert. At three o'clock, coffee and fresh-baked cake. At six, a slice of farmer's bread with a bit of cheese or sausage.

She also gave me personal freedom, trusting me to comport myself like a respectable young woman on walks from her apartment to the old city centre of Nürnberg, where I would spend an afternoon exploring in a manner befitting a lady. I thought I had done a bang-up job. I bought a few shirts for the upcoming school year, visited a bookstore and pretended to browse the titles with interest, and sat in a pew of the Lorenz Kirche and practiced looking dour and saintly. I didn't set one foot in the red-light district, even though I knew exactly how to get there. I didn't eat any street food; Omi made it clear that it was meant to be eaten only during the Christmas market, when all manner of public consumption was allowed. I walked home feeling very adult and noble. At the corner store, I saw a display for 'Coke Light'. We'd had Diet Coke in the States for a while, but it was new for Germans. They'd retooled it to appeal to Europeans; the can was a pale blue, accented by yellow. In small type, there was a little exclamatory message, *'Mit Zitrone!'* accompanied by a picture of a lemon. It was worth a try.

I enjoyed the soda on my short trip from the market to my grandmother's, remarking at the pleasant bite of the citrus, swinging my shopping bag in time with my step. I fished the apartment key from my pants and made for the lock when the door swung open. Omi took one look at the open container in my hand and smacked me. 'Drinking! On the street! From a can! Walking *and* drinking from a can!'

I could see the table set for coffee and noticed that it was already 4 p.m. She'd made a small cake, enough for two. The coffee sat in a beautiful porcelain pot with two cups waiting and a bowl of freshly whipped cream snuggled up to it. There was no tea for me; Omi thought I was ready for adult fare. And here I was, face stinging from her slap, drinking soda from a can like a harlot, insensitive to the magic hour when we should have been spending time with each other savouring cake and sipping strong coffee. I didn't begrudge her the smack; it was a direct way of expressing her hurt that I understood immediately. I'd much rather that than passing an uncomfortably silent evening with a passive-aggressive octogenarian. Also, it was better than some of the other punishments she's meted out, namely, trying to bring down my sister at a full sprint with a wooden cheeseboard used as a boomerang. Sandy most probably had been abusing me and I'd ratted her out. As Sandy went tearing down the hall toward her bedroom, Omi sent the cheese platter spinning in hot pursuit. It slammed into the closet at the end of the hallway, just missing Sandy's head and leaving a nasty gash in the wood, leading me to believe that my grandmother wasn't beyond maiming her own grandchildren in the cause of justice. It could have been much worse.

I spent the rest of the summer conscious of time, looking forward to performing our three o'clock choreography in her small kitchen. I collected the plates and set the table. She rinsed the coffeepot with scalding water and ground the beans. We'd have made a cake together or I would bring one from a trip into town. She told me stories of the war and of my grandfather. And I listened and enjoyed 3 p.m. as I never had as a child.

When I returned home to Virginia, Mom and I started our own choreography. We had to steal time from our American lives, where 3 p.m. sat squarely in the middle of the local custom for hectic extracurricular activity until dinner. But we managed to conjure some magic, setting aside the organic and whole wheat for something scrumptious. Sometimes we shared thoughts and stories. Mostly we sat silently, enjoying each other's company and savouring small cakes, preferably something laced with almond, and a cup of strong coffee.

Making 3 p.m. happen for the people who live in Montpelier is a living memory of my Omi and my mother. It's a natural inclination for many people to decompress and treat themselves as the day comes to a close. Before you have to go home and make dinner for your family but after you've given blood at the office, sneaking away in the late afternoon is one of life's great pleasures. At my shop, it's a respected ritual.

Ann said to me today that she couldn't quite figure out what it was about our store because it wasn't just a store. There was something like home about it. She comes in every day, sometimes twice a day, and I'll see her sitting at the window with a latte and a piece of cake. Then Anne will join her, and Kyle will come around and sit to make a threesome. And they'll sip and eat and laugh. Occasionally I'll even pour myself a cup of coffee and join them. I said to her, that what I had always wanted was to bring 3 p.m. to America. Where coffee and cake weren't inhaled but savoured with a lovely setting and kind people. 'Yes. That's it. That's what it feels like,' she said.

We talk about nothing in particular, we nibble at dense, fudgy chocolate hearts, and we enjoy each other's company. So while the women who acquainted me with this ceremony are gone, I'm here in the Green Mountains making sure that it lives on at 3 p.m. on the dot. Don't be late.

Mandelhoernchen

WHEN I STAYED with my grandmother those many summers ago, she and I went to the corner pastry shop the day before I left to stock up on *mandelhoernchen* to take back to the States to share with my mom at 3 p.m.

My mother missed innumerable things from Germany – the cobblestone streets and the hourly church bells, the Christmas markets and the language. But I could bring this one thing home for her.

MAKES 48 COOKIES

2 pounds almond paste
1 cup sugar
5 large egg whites
Bread flour for rolling and shaping
8 ounces sliced blanched almonds, lightly
    crushed
Simple syrup (see Note)

Combine the almond paste and sugar in the bowl of an electric mixer fitted with the paddle attachment. Add the egg whites, incorporating them gradually to avoid lumps. Continue to mix at medium speed, scraping down the sides of the bowl as needed, until you have a smooth paste.

Lightly flour the work surface and your hands. Divide the paste into 3 equal pieces. Roll each piece into a 20-inch log, using just enough flour to keep the paste from sticking to the table. Cut each log into 16 equal pieces.

Place the almonds on a sheet of baking paper or on a halfsheet pan. Roll each of the small dough pieces in the almonds, at the same time shaping them into small logs. Be sure that the almonds adhere all around; you might have to roll the pieces in your hands first to eliminate excess flour, which will prevent the almonds from sticking. Transfer the logs to the floured table and continue rolling the pieces between your palms and the table until each one is 5 inches long, with slightly tapered ends.

Line a sheet pan with parchment paper. Bend the pieces into horseshoe shapes 2½ inches wide and place them on the pan. Allow the cookies to dry at room temperature for a few hours.

Bake, double panned (two sheet pans together to protect the bottoms from over browning), at 375°F/190°C for approximately 15 minutes or until golden brown and baked through. Brush simple syrup over the cookies immediately after removing them from the oven. After they have cooled completely, dip the ends into melted dark chocolate.

Baker's Note: Simple syrup is liquid sugar. To make it, combine 1 cup sugar and 1 cup water in a microwavable bowl. Microwave for 5 minutes on high and then stir. Continue to microwave 1 minute at a time until the sugar is completely dissolved.

Chapter Sixteen

Chocolate-Covered Chakras

4 p.m.

I'M IMPATIENT. We're sneaking up on the end of my workday and I've finished every conceivable pastry task I can think of. Now I want to close so I can go running, wrestle with the dogs, make dinner, and relax with Ray, and then start off fresh in the morning and play with sugar again.

I've given up any pretence that I've developed into a serene adult, someone who can be still. I have trouble breathing deeply and thoughtfully; there's no calming my mind and meditating on nothingness. My chakras are not thoughtfully aligned and evenly spread, resulting in a well-adjusted, patient mien. Mine are tightly bundled and chocolate-coated, resulting in a scattered woman always itching to do something new, *now*. And I'm always itching for pastries, to eat them or bake them or invent them. I'll push aside even the most pressing engagement to get down and dirty with sugar and butter.

Even during winter exam week in college, when I knew I had to start cracking the books. I was having trouble staving off a growing compulsion to build a giant gingerbread village. It had been needling at me, this desire, since I detected the first hint of chill in the air. And every time I pretended to care about Adam Smith and his *Wealth of Nations*, I'd drift into a flour-dusted daydream.

I broke down and abandoned any prospect of infusing my brain with knowledge. I hightailed it out of the library and spent every last cent of food money and the little I had saved for Christmas presents on molasses, flour, and a boatload of expensive spices. I loitered about the candy aisle, fussing over whether Necco wafers or nonpareils would make better roof shingles. I discovered it was nonpareils, hands down. I cleaned the poker chips off our dining room table and scrubbed off a year of beer residue and nacho cheese. I overlapped pieces of parchment so the entire wood veneer surface was covered. I spent a few hours tracing templates onto paper for the walls, roof, shutters, and door. When the gingerbread came out of the oven, I transferred it to the dining table, laid the templates on top, and cut very precisely. Once everything cooled, I mortared the walls together with royal icing, keeping them steady with soup cans until everything set. As I was lowering the roof panels onto the village's town hall, my roommates started to trickle in. They were inured to my sideshows and stopped only to steal a piece of candy or instruct me that a clock tower was listing a little too far to the right.

I finished, just after midnight. Royal icing dripped off of every surface. My hands cramped from the intricate detail work and my fingers were in such deep spasm, I couldn't let go of the tweezers I'd used to place little pearls of sanding sugar on the rooflines to add sparkle.

I had two exams in the morning. I fell asleep, economic and comparative religion texts open on my chest and flour in my hair.

This wasn't an extraordinary episode. My best friend, Christine, and I would regularly leave class midlecture, having spent a half hour passing notes to each other: 'Hey, let's blow this joint and make some cheesecake!' We'd run home and crank up the oven. We'd often engage in an intellectual dialectic regarding pastries and their valuable properties, wondering aloud whether a cheesecake was meant to rise a half foot past its container and shouldn't we stop it from exploding in the oven?

Pre-Starbucks and espresso bars, we still wanted a little Euro coffee house vibe to go with our hooky pastries. So we invested in a fine selection of powdered International Foods instant coffees, Swiss Vanilla being the perennial favourite, took our sweet time in its preparation, and sat down in the late afternoon for cake and coffee.

For a long while these memories have made me antsy for Germany and her pastries. I need to shut down the shop for a solid block of time and go hug my family and eat some cake. The last time I spent any quality time in Europe was with Christine, right after college.

We visited Salzburg, my first hometown. We dropped by the Café Tomaselli, in an open square of the Goldgasse. We had coffee and a morsel. We set off on foot down the road and peeked into Mozart's childhood home – low ceilings, tiny harpsichord, but no pastries. It took about five minutes to see everything worth seeing. Back on the street, Christine and I both spied a cosy café right across from us. It was on the second floor, red geraniums gushing out of the flower boxes at the windows. Poetic-looking young men, cigarettes dangling from their mouths, perused newspapers bound together with old-fashioned wooden dowels along the seams so they could be hung back up at the front door for the next bohemian.

It was irresistible and we insisted on going in. Another cup of coffee couldn't hurt. We sat, ordered a *großer brauner* (a generous serving of strong coffee with heavy whipped cream) and, almost as an afterthought, said, 'What the hell! Let's get some cake.' And so it went, from the Café Fürst, which we had to visit because it is the birthplace of Mozart's balls. That is, the little chocolate named after Mozart, filled with marzipan, pistachio paste, and nougat and covered in chocolate. You haven't been to Salzburg unless you've had a handful. And onto the Café Sacher, the cousin to the original and more famous Viennese institution; it still was *the* place to get a piece of sacher torte. Then to Café Glockenspiel, a prime people-watching outfit facing the statue of Mozart with a lovely view of Mozart Square. And when we thought we were done, I realised we hadn't been to Niemetz. Tucked behind the horse well, next to the Festival Halle and conveniently close to where we had parked the car, Café Niemetz was where my mother took us as kids most often. It was the hangout of singers and musicians and housed some great childhood memories.

I couldn't be denied such a nostalgic trip. And these wonderful cakes – the deep, slightly bitter chocolates and the voluptuous coating of marzipan over delicate layers of a torte – they opened my eyes to what had been missing from my American life. I'd been completely assimilated into Yankee dessert culture, carpet-bombed with corn syrup missiles fuelled with hydrogenated soybean oil and red dye #2. No wonder my mother kept that crap out of the house when there was such pure bounty to be had across the ocean. She had told me childhood stories of hiding among the dark pews of her hometown cathedral, the Lorenz Kirche, and savouring a *mandelhoernchen* from the local baker while she pored over her worn copy of Kierkegaard's *Fear and Trembling*. I had always taken the story as proof of my mother's dietetic hypocrisy, that she was allowed sweet indulgences as a child while I was denied.

But now I saw that she understood the value of forbearance, because if it's truly worth having you can wait. And in reality, my mom wasn't completely withholding in the desserts department; she just thought they had a time and place, and they had to be beautifully made and with patience. My mother was anything but impatient.

Christmas time was a well-planned orgiastic festival of butter cookies and cinnamon stars. Easter was fertile with chocolate eggs and those beautifully rendered, lifelike Easter bunnies. And on birthdays, she became a baking sorceress, creating cakes and tasty party favours my American friends never imagined. She spent months leading up to the big day planning and consulting, asking what type of cake I was leaning toward and what type of party favour I'd like for the table. She created lush flower arrangements, daisy-shaped sugar cookies on Popsicle-stick stems, for the centrepiece. She sculpted woodland creatures from almond paste and arranged them around the flowers. And the cake was always beautifully homemade, filled with bittersweet chocolate, European butter, and free-range eggs.

But she never, ever made these things outside of the confines of the prescribed occasion. And me with my pastry impatience, I couldn't understand what the big deal was. Why couldn't I have a nice *butterzeug* in the heat of summer? Or a slice of layer cake for an afternoon snack? Why hold back on me and make me wait?

Dessert for my mother was sacred. It wasn't an afterthought, a procrastination ploy, or a craving but the pinnacle of great celebration and a pure expression of love. For her, the sweets I wanted every day ruined my appreciation for the weighty and potentially dangerous magic of sugar. She harnessed it for the grand gesture, while I was looking to dilute it into its base parts for an impatient fix. The impact of her message didn't go unheard, but I was still too young to appreciate its full substance; I wanted the magic, no matter how diluted and impure, whenever I was feeling antsy for it.

It took a while but I'd come full circle. Standing in the middle of a busy Getreidegasse in Salzburg, a young woman with a grotesquely distended stomach packed with an army of desserts, I began to understand my mother's truly high regard for pastry and why it's wise to practice restraint and patience. In no small part because I felt terribly sick. And right now, a slightly older woman standing in my very own bakery, although I'm still impatient when it comes to the details of my own life, I've learned to bring a bit of stoicism to baking for my neighbours, because I want to create the grand gesture born of patience and love that will become a treasured memory, just as my mother did for me.

Apfelkuchen

OMI MADE AN *apfelkuchen* for afternoon coffee when I was hiding in Germany after college. She, like me, had ants in the pants. She whipped up this cake in less than an hour. But here's one of the drawbacks of suffering bouts of antsy: she whipped it up so quickly that she folded a fly into the batter. That requires some major speed and impatience. So while this cake works in a pinch if you're antsy for a delicious dessert fast, just take a little time to avoid incorporating wildlife into the mix.

MAKES ONE 8-INCH CAKE

For the batter

11 tablespoons (1 stick plus 3 tablespoons) unsalted butter, plus additional for greasing the pan and sautéing the apples

8 apples (Granny Smith or an equally tart and firm apple), peeled, cored, and sliced

Juice of 1 lemon

1½ tablespoons Calvados (apple brandy)

⅔ cup sugar

2 large eggs

1 teaspoon vanilla extract

1 cup all-purpose flour

½ teaspoon salt

1 teaspoon baking powder

For the glaze

1 cup confectioners' sugar

½ teaspoon vanilla extract

2 tablespoons milk

FOR THE BATTER

Preheat the oven to 350°F/180°C. Butter an 8-inch round cake pan and line it with buttered parchment paper.

Sprinkle the apples with lemon juice. Melt an extra knob of butter in a large skillet. Sauté the apples with the Calvados, tossing occasionally, until golden, about 5 minutes.

Place the butter and sugar in the bowl of an electric mixer fitted with the whisk attachment; cream on high until fluffy. On slow, add the eggs one at a time, then the vanilla. Slowly add the flour, salt, and baking powder, mixing until just combined.

Transfer the batter to the prepared pan. Smooth

the batter and arrange the apples on top in a circular pattern.

Bake for 60 to 75 minutes until the batter is browned and is springy. (I don't know how Omi managed to make this in an hour because mine always takes longer.)

FOR THE GLAZE

While the cake is baking, combine the confectioners' sugar, vanilla, and milk in a small bowl. Whisk until smooth.

Gently brush the glaze over the *apfelkuchen* when it is almost cool but still a little warm. Then allow the cake to cool completely. *Mahlzeit!*

Chapter Seventeen

And Did I Mention We Were on the Food Network?

5 p.m.

WE RECEIVED A VISIT from a camera crew. It was on Monday, when we close early, so no one was the wiser in town. I put on a clean shirt and took my hair out of a ponytail. We'd been cleaning the kitchen for weeks in anticipation. Tim and I even scrubbed the glass of the oven doors. They were going to be on TV too.

The last time I was on television it was a local news thing. Not as fancy as the Food Network. We hadn't opened the store to the public yet and I was still sleeping, exercising, and sitting down to eat. Just a little puff piece, human-interest stuff. My macaroons had been featured in *In Style* magazine, and that was a minor deal in these parts.

A reporter and a cameraman came by. Asked me a few questions. Had me talk about my macaroons and the other delights I'd be offering in my shop.

Reporter: 'So, your macaroons. They aren't the usual coconut we're all used to? They're almond? No coconut at all?'

Idiot (me): 'That's right! They're traditional French almond macaroons. NO coconut WHATSOEVER. Just almonds, COCONUT, sugar, and egg whites.'

If you listen very carefully to the tape of my pathetic news debut, you can hear Ray in the background laughing his ass off.

Moving on, our intrepid reporter broached the elephant in the room. Hollywood.

'So, now that you've moved from your glitzy life in la-la land to quiet Vermont, should we be looking out for an influx of Hollywood visitors?'

And I didn't think twice; I didn't think. I just answered with honesty and my usual utter lack of tact and charm.

'*Oh, God, I hope not!*'

This is when I choose to be natural on camera: my face squirrelly and filled with disgust, spitting out my dread at the thought of my old life descending on the quiet of Vermont.

I can't take a decent still either. There's a little write-up in a local magazine with a picture of me holding some pastries. I knew Ray was looking at the article when I heard him howling with laughter in the back of the store.

'I've never seen you smile quite like that.' He's very tactful. Unlike his wife.

'I know. I was muttering under my breath the entire time.'

And if you know this and you take a look at that picture, you probably have a good shot at guessing what I was saying. As a matter of fact, I think I was up to a word that rhymes with 'plucking' in my mantra 'take the plucking picture already' when the flash went off.

In the past, with each successive mention in a local paper or a national magazine, we'd get a respectable bump in business. A few more people than usual asking to see me in person; a few more stickies of doom; a few more trips to the office supply store for Post-its. And then we'd settle back into our comfortable groove, having added a couple regulars to our family but nothing we couldn't handle with good cheer, great pastry, and strong coffee.

But a visit from the Food Network, that's what every small food business dreams about. And the experience of being on camera, of constantly smiling and simultaneously baking, it wasn't half bad. The hosts were charming, even when the cameras weren't rolling. The crew was lovely and respectful of our shop. And everyone brought a degree of enthusiasm to the endeavour that shocked me because I was so used to the 'seen it, done it' attitude that travels with movie crews. These people were genuinely excited about food. And they were excited about food in Vermont. And about telling the world about food in Vermont. That made it easy to do something I'd never imagined doing – being in front of a camera. It's easy to share something, even in front of millions of people, if you love what you do.

Getting in front of those millions of the food obsessed also gives you a huge spike in business. At such a perilous economic time, with food prices up 50 per cent for most of our core ingredients, gas prices affecting everything else, and our entire economy in an official recession, it's a miracle that anyone is making ends meet. This kind of exposure could be the difference between making it another year or closing down after Christmas.

It also translates into thousands of macaroon orders, keeping me in the shop long after we close. High school kids cram into the kitchen after class, helping me scoop and filling the hot bakery with spastic energy. The shop is filled to the rafters with customers who've come from all over the country and beyond, even at those hours when we used to have a restful lull. Our regulars are getting pushed to the side, waiting in line when they've never had to before. Ann's popping into the back with a cocktail shaker, to take the edge off. I don't sit down at three for coffee anymore.

I'm so inundated with work that I'm no longer capable of complex thoughts; I exist on a mental plane filled with white oven noise and the smell of ground almonds. And though our sales are up, way up, we have to hire more people to keep up with the demand. Which pretty much evens out any financial gains we could make.

I'm also getting emails from home bakers who've seen me on television, exclaiming their deep passion for the floured arts. They want to know how I did it, how did I open such a lovely shop without schooling or experience in such things. They want to take the plunge too, maybe get their chance of being on the Food Network!

I don't answer these emails for fear of stomping on such high hopes.

Because the answer is quite simple: *don't do it!* And don't use me as a guide; I'm not a good influence. My story isn't uplifting and inspirational. I had meant to go to school for this stuff. Really. But my baking took on a life of its own, and it just happened. If I could do it again, I'd get my ignorant self educated. Because someone at some point would have said to me, 'You know, if you go out on your own and open a bakery, you're not allowed to sleep.' At the very least I would have learned how to manage such a place. So my first instinct is to tell that home baker with the big dream that they should hold fast to the joy they receive in baking for pleasure. And if they must pursue a career in it, go to school. Or work in a hard-core bakery, where the hours are abysmal and the production is monumental. Don't mortgage your life to bake unless you know what the hell you're doing. And be careful what you wish for, because while being on TV can give you unprecedented business and exposure, it can also sap you of any will to live and increase your daily grey hair count astronomically. That lady you saw on TV, wearing make-up and a clean shirt, that person doesn't exist. I just brought her out for a few minutes to appear on the little screen; ten minutes after the camera crew left, she transformed back into a baking pumpkin.

We're asked, 'Are you going to expand? Open more stores? Go national?' But the only relevant question is, 'Are you going crazy? And if not, when?' Because this is painful; no one tells you how much it hurts when you succeed. You hear about the failures and how it sucks to lose your dream to low sales figures and bad management. But no one tells you about the travails of having your business double overnight or quadruple or more, because this can cause failure as well. If we don't live up to the demand from this exposure, we can't count on getting another break to prove ourselves a second time. So we've got to make it work right now, and that means I have to stay here all night if that's what it takes to get these orders out.

But when this insanity isn't bringing me to the brink of sobs, I'm as close to Buddha under the bodhi as I'll ever be, just without the sitting still. Because I'm doing what I was meant to do, and every once in a while I'll eat a stray macaroon. And they're damn tasty. Buddha never had it so good. And I'll tell the home bakers with big pastry dreams, that it is possible. It may kill you, strip you of sanity and finances, but it can also be rewarding. And sometimes – and those times may be few and far between – sometimes it is nirvana.

Passionfruit Healer

I TRIED THIS COCKTAIL for the first time in Buenos Aires. Ray and I went for Christmas for two whole weeks of vacation. A hemisphere away from mile-high snowdrifts and unintentional power slides on black ice. No waking at 3:30 a.m. and to bed at 8 p.m. We ate dinner at midnight. I rode some hyperactive horses with genuine gauchos. We'd have a cocktail to pass the time while we mulled the wine list. I exposed my ankles to the sun and ate grilled meat for breakfast. But what I took back with me as my fondest taste memory was this beautiful concoction.

When we've got two seconds to relax and have a cocktail, this little number brings back the ease of Buenos Aires. It's tropical, mysterious, and a great healer.

MAKES TWO SERVINGS

A few fresh mint leaves

A drop or two of ginger extract

12 ounces white cranberry juice

8 ounces lemon vodka

2 tablespoons Triple Sec

12 ounces passionfruit juice

Muddle the mint leaves, ginger extract to taste, and a touch of the white cranberry juice in the bottom of a serving pitcher to release the oil in the mint leaves. Ginger extract is potent stuff, so start out timidly. Add the vodka, Triple Sec, passionfruit juice, and remaining cranberry juice. Stir and add ice. Serve in large glasses and behold a miraculous recovery.

Chapter Eighteen

Running Regrets

6 p.m.

WHEN I'M DONE BAKING and we're closed, I run. In the spring, through summer, and into fall, I take a right outside of our shop and hightail it down Route 12. I follow the river past the nature centre, toward the town of Worcester. In the winter, I'm on the treadmill at home. This is my time to think, to remember what it is I've surely forgotten during a long, flour-coated day and to talk to my mom. Along with baking, running is one of the great legacies she left me.

In 1995, I was standing in the hallway outside of the bathroom, my forehead resting against the doorjamb,

when my mom called to tell me she had colon cancer;
I started softly knocking my head against the wood to
stop from crying. She had been hedging her health bets
all her life: restricting her diet, exercising, abstaining
from alcohol, driving cautiously. At first they thought
it was just a minor abnormality, a polyp. Maybe even
haemorrhoids. I laughed because anything vaguely
defective in my mother's health was impossible. She
was a superhero! She ate whole grains with glee and
slurped wheatgrass like fine wine. And she was a
marathon runner.

Mom had taken up running after I made one of
those gracious remarks that are the staple of preteen
mother-daughter conversation.

'Why do your arms jiggle like that?'

She was making a left-hand turn into a gas station.
The hand-over-hand motion highlighted a barely
discernible looseness in her triceps. As she was gassing
the car, just the midsection of her body visible from
the passenger seat, I saw her pinch herself up and
down her arm, assessing the damage of time, smarting
from my cruel comment.

She started by running a few quarter-mile laps
around the block. Despite my valuation of her
physique, she looked great. She was thin and leggy.
Back then she had a belt that really said it all. 'Foxy
Lady!' My sister's high school suitors timed their visits
to coincide with Mom's launch from the backyard.

'You sure you and Sandy aren't sisters, Mrs. Bullock?' The neighbourhood gents were especially pleased by her new exercise regimen and found time to manicure their lawns and prune hedges, all the while yelling their encouragement.

'Looking good, Helga! Keep it up!'

I was less supportive and found her public sweating mortifying. She wore tiny, shiny running shorts. Not to mention she'd wear lipstick, and her coif moved with a luxuriant Prell bounce.

She ran the same streets alone, over and over.

'Why don't you run somewhere else for a change? It's embarrassing.'

When my mother was diagnosed, my first thought was that she'd have to stop running. That would be a loss to both her and our neighbourhood. But she turned her back on running and her past pursuits at securing a long life. She grasped on to the tragedy in the pronouncement and carried it with her. Her fight, it seems, had been in the prevention, the supplements and the exercise regimens. The leafy greens and organic reds. It was all for naught and she'd lost. There's always a chance that someone will pull through, go triumphantly into remission, but you can't depend on it. And the stories you hear – the ones where the feisty lady clenches her fists and cries, 'I'm not going to let it get me! I'm going to fight this and win!' – that wasn't my mom.

She did, however, have a score to settle and wanted company doing it. She was ready to open her mind and her digestive tract, because she didn't know how long she'd have use of either. So after she was diagnosed she ate everything: dairy, meat, a couple of fillet-o-fishes. Boy, was she pissed for denying herself for so many years. It was an epic food bender.

Coffee and cake found itself on the daily docket. There were restaurants that needed to be visited. She kept reviews and made a detailed list for my father. Get a reservation; we don't have a lot of time. My mother was known for her palate; nothing of her own making ever passed her lips that had an artificial ingredient, so she recognised the chemical components to the atom when she ate out. Her greatest praise of a restaurant meal was that it tasted 'clean'. When we set out to sample wedding cakes for my upcoming nuptials because we'd be too busy to make our own, she dissected the alleged buttercream we were proffered and announced in no uncertain terms, 'This isn't buttercream!' and then rattled off what she surmised it was. And she was dead on.

The Inn at Little Washington was highest on her list of culinary destinations. Veal, goose fat, oxtail consommé, she was up for the challenge. She was even willing to eat their desserts, although they'd pale in comparison to her own handiwork.

My mother and father spent a long weekend at the

inn and took every meal there. She recalled minor culinary details with awe, from breakfast to dinner. She ate each morsel and ventured with a threatening fork into Dad's plate more than once. She thought the whole experience, to quote my grandmother's greatest compliment, 'vunderfohl'. She went so far as to buy the cookbook sold by the inn. That was high praise indeed, from my mother.

We went out to dinner on New Year's Eve, to the venerable Hay-Adams Hotel in the heart of D.C. New Year's had been a holiday kept well within my mother's controlling hands – the meal, the entertainment, and the alcohol all of her choosing. She'd cook and bake for days, arrange an elaborate buffet in the dining room. She would orchestrate the downstairs for the *feuerzangenbowle,* the traditional German flaming punch, making sure that the table and the immediate environs weren't flammable. And the entertainment was easily arranged. The guests were all opera singers or musicians. Everyone would sidle up to the piano, sheet music in hand, drunkenly duelling each other with high Cs and maddening breath control. Sandy and I would cringe in the corner waiting for an intermission from the noise or for dessert to be served, whichever came first. But my mother always saved the best for last. The lights would dim, someone would push 'play' on the audio, and she'd appear at the top of the steps wearing sheer gauze harem pants, a scarf festooned with tinkling coins tied at the waist, and a tiny bustier embroidered with more of the same racket-making coins. She'd descend slowly, castanets clacking away in her hands, and when she hit the bottom of the stairs, Salome's Dance of the Seven Veils would begin. To my utter horror.

My mother hadn't put on that particular belly dancing show in some time, not since her muscled abdomen had been left with foot-long scars from surgery and certainly not since she consented, under much protestation, to getting a colostomy bag. So this year we sat at the beautiful table in the restored dining room of the Hay-Adams, conservatively dressed, drinking Champagne, and enjoying, not a great meal, but a lovely meal nonetheless. She might, at one point in her cancer-free life, have proclaimed the meal unclean in parts, but she wasn't wasting time seeking out the unpleasant anymore and stuck to the tastes that made her happy.

We spent hours together rifling through recipes, some scribbled on loose paper in old German script and others ripped from the food section of the *Washington Post*. She considered their relative merits and put aside those that she felt I had to have. *Butterzeug*, the butter cookies she made every year at Christmas, always heart shaped. Sandy and I would sneak onto the side porch where she kept them stored in tins in the cool air and eat as many as we could before we got frostbitten.

Zwetschgendatschi, the beloved plum tart of childhood. New York cheesecake, the closest to Lindy's she could reverse engineer. Her famous Pecan Chocolate Torte, also known as the Orgasm Cake. She handed them to me resolutely. I have them, still sitting in a box, unopened. There are some recipes that I memorised, never needing to consult her handwritten notes. But for those that I haven't, whenever I go to the box to find them, I get sucked into her handwriting and the memory of her. The loops and slashes of the letters still bearing the shape of her German grade school lessons are living pieces of her. Like the outgoing message we can't erase but dare not play. Or the cassettes of her singing.

There are some recipes I can't make because I'd rather have her make them.

Our last task was to visit Germany before she was too sick to make the trip. We visited Nürnberg, her hometown, and the most famous German Christmas market, the *Christkindlsmarkt*. We ate small lard-packed and darkly browned bratwurst sausages nestled side by side on a hard white roll. We smothered them with spicy mustard and walked among the stalls, taking in the handcrafts and merriment, stopping for *glühwein*, a warm, sweet mulled wine, to warm up between bites, and then finishing up with a *lebkuchen*, the Nürnberger spice cake.

We visited our family in Bergen nestled in

the Bavarian Alps and walked slowly up the neighbourhood peak, Hochfelln. At the top, we settled into worn wooden benches and had coffee and cake, *Kaiserschmarrn* and *topfenstrudel*, Alpine sugar bombs both. In Germany, cafés sit atop every treacherous mountain, making the most gruelling ascent worth every blister and curse because you sit with the most breathtaking view at three thousand feet in a cosy cottage with warm food and a cold beer. So often, I'll make a painful physical journey to a beautiful place in America and lament the absence of these things that I find sacred.

Decades after her first marathon and five years after her diagnosis, when my mother lay dying of cancer, I took care of her. We'd spend time in the early morning, visiting while she made her way through a tower of pills. When she fell into a narcotic doze, I'd watch her with profound regret.

So I started running her route while she slept. I didn't have her stunning road presence, just a ponytail and sloppy shorts, but I wanted to honour her by running in circles and to honour her life, and as I bounced along the pavement of my childhood I kept reminding myself to live without regret and with love.

Now that she's gone, I still run and think of her. And every year at Thanksgiving and Christmas time, when my mother broke out her culinary genius and let go of all things healthy, Sandy and I will start trading calls if we aren't spending the holidays together. The conversation is always the same.' Okay, so I have the fingerling potatoes, the mayo, and the shallots. I know I also need oil. What am I forgetting?' There are recipes that were never written down: for the potato salad we had on Christmas Eve along with marinated white asparagus and the Nürnberger bratwurst we smuggled in from Germany in little lard-packed cans in the summer; or the Thanksgiving gravy my mother and my aunt would conjure from the drippings of the bird; or the exact range of spices she used to dress the bird to make it so flavourful and crisp. We'll never remember them without each other's help. So we talk to each other at least five times in the day to consult about ingredients and to report back the results. While we always do a good job, we also know that it will never taste as good as Mom's. And we agree that we'd never want it to be any other way. She gave us so much in the way of love and memories. And when she broke out the good stuff, eschewing the lean and the green fibre-packed roughage to bring out the fatty food of celebration, her love shone as bright as the star of Bethlehem.

I'm always mindful of my mother, remembering to enjoy the good stuff and share it with others. To run like a kid, not because it's good for me but because it brings me joy. When I get back, sweaty and happy, we lock up and take stock of our day. Ray will open a bottle of wine and I'll take the lid off the cookie jar. Ray pours everyone a small glass and we toast. I've trained everyone in the awkward ways of German drinking: you've got to make eye contact with each person as you clink glasses. To do otherwise, you not only disrespect your drinking partner, you'll be cursed with seven years of bad sex. And while everyone giggles and still protests at having to lock eyes with each toast, they've acknowledged that they've brought the tradition into their lives outside of work.

As we scrub, organise, and gossip, we make dibs on any pastries that are left over and fight over the last drop in the wine bottle. When we're done, I kick everyone out the side door, locking it tight, making sure they remember their pastries. I turn off the lights, turn on the alarm, and make a mad dash for the front door.

I wave to Gayle; she's leaning over the railing that leads up to Terry's and smoking a cigarette, enjoying a moment of peace when there's no one in their store. I head toward home and the winding hills of Worcester, to our tiny house with a gravel driveway lined with maple, a barn tucked off to one side and miles of rolling hills we can call our very own.

When I turn into the drive, the dogs race out to greet me, playing chicken with my mud encrusted Subaru as I make my way into the barn. Ray's beaten me home and started the grill. We stand outside with our pups running circles around us, and we marvel at our luck. Dumpling Hill to our back, Worcester Range to our front, and pines all around. And in the background, a distant owl calls to us and welcomes us home.

Helga's Cake

WHEN WE FIRST OPENED, even though I wasn't a big
fan of the Orgasm Cake as a kid, I emailed my
aunt Erika for my mom's recipe. She sent it along
with a little note: 'Dear Gesine, I understand if you
won't be able to call the pecan chocolate torte 'the
Orgasm Cake' if you are selling it at the store – you
might end up with another line out the front door
like at the opening!'

I looked it over a few times. I did some
calculations to increase the recipe from a single
cake to wholesale quantities without screwing
up the texture, then set about whipping eggs and
grinding nuts, enjoying the dark aromas coming
off the pecans as they got ground in the processor.
I'd made a lot of German tortes in my pastry shop,
mostly nut-based affairs from recipes I'd collected as
an adult. I'd never bothered to look at my mother's
recipe until that moment. It was deeply rooted in
German baking but used an all-American nut. When
it came out of the oven, it was light and springy, like
a boring sponge cake, but it gave off a beautiful and
complex scent of roasted nuts and caramel. Before
I made the icing, I tried a piece of the cake naked

and warm. Damn. It was a complicated piece of goodness. It was almost savoury; the pecans gave it a depth and texture that defied the underlying sweetness. And when you add the chocolate buttercream, that's a sensual piece of cake. Because I sell it at the store, I had to agree with Tante Erika, it couldn't keep its original name. So now it's called Helga's Cake. I like that a lot better.

MAKES ONE 8-INCH THREE LAYERED CAKE

For the cake
Nonstick cooking spray
12 ounces pecans
1 cup sugar
½ teaspoon salt
8 large eggs, separated, plus 2 whole eggs
1 tablespoon vanilla extract
2 teaspoons baking powder

For the buttercream
12 ounces bittersweet chocolate, finely chopped
8 large egg yolks
2 teaspoons vanilla extract
½ cup hot coffee or boiling water
½ pound (2 sticks) unsalted butter, at room
  temperature

FOR THE CAKE

Preheat the oven to 325°F/170°C. Lightly grease three 8-inch round cake pans with 1½-inch sides. Line the bottoms of the pans with wax paper and lightly grease the paper.

In a food processor, grind the pecans with ½ cup of the sugar and the salt until they turn into a fine meal. Add the egg yolks, 2 whole eggs, vanilla, and baking powder and blend until you get a smooth paste.

Whip the 8 egg whites on high in the bowl of an electric mixer using the whisk attachment. Just as the egg whites start to gain volume and look white and fluffy (but not chunky), add the remaining ½ cup sugar in a slow, steady stream. Whisk on high until the whites are very shiny and hold a stiff peak.

Transfer the pecan paste to a large metal mixing bowl and stir in a heaping spoonful of the egg whites to lighten the batter. Gently fold the remaining egg whites into the pecan mixture until well incorporated, being careful to keep the integrity of the aerated eggs. Divide the batter among the three cake pans and bake for 30 to 45 minutes, until the cake springs back when you touch it. Allow to cool completely on wire racks before you release from the pan.

FOR THE BUTTERCREAM

Place the chocolate, egg yolks, and vanilla in a blender or food processor. With the motor running, add the coffee in a slow, steady stream. Add the butter in small bits and process until the frosting is smooth. If it's too soft to spread, refrigerate.

This is a strange method of making buttercream. I've tried it in a more traditional manner, using a water bath and a mixer, but it really doesn't come out the same.

TO ASSEMBLE THE CAKE

You know how to do it by now. First layer, then buttercream. Add the second layer, more buttercream. You've got it.

Chapter Nineteen

Career Day

I T'S CAREER DAY at Main Street School. Amelia asked me to come. She's twelve but has a delivery so low and seasoned you'd think you were in the presence of a chain-smoking forties-era movie siren and not a reed of a girl. She comes in with her girlfriends after tennis practice for an Italian soda and to flirt with Ray.

I sit alongside an attorney who moonlights as a legislative lobbyist, a surgeon, our city manager, a cellist, and a paramedic who had the foresight to bring along Chuck, a cuddly search and rescue dog. We're facing a group of fifty hormonal tweeners. Our job is to get them all kinds of excited about working. We're screwed.

The paramedic and the surgeon are up first. Both have high-stress, life-altering jobs. Blood! Entrails! It's juicy stuff. We're getting some signs of life from the audience. The paramedic gestures to fluffy Chuck like he's a showroom Mercedes: 'And I get to work with puppies!' The attorney and city manager both straighten their ties and come out like duelling banjos, detailing their sound educational backgrounds and vast civic contributions. Taxes! Legislation! The kids slip back into unconsciousness. The cellist, a rangy, awkward-looking man in a tea-stained T-shirt and rust-coloured jeans, takes a deep, shuddering breath and readies himself to give what appears to be a prepared speech. He reveals in reverential tones that while he's a professional cellist, he will never stop taking lessons. Ever. He has calculated the hours a week he spends practicing his instrument and gravely details the ratio of money spent for continued lessons versus revenue generated from paying gigs to illustrate the low profit margins facing a working musician. So a kid asks him, 'But this is what you always wanted to do, right? Being a musician was your dream job?'

Our sad cellist shakes his head morosely. 'Nope. Wanted to be a BMX racer.'

Not one of these men can say he is working in his dream job. Everyone but the cellist dreamed of rock-and-roll stardom. Now *I'm* depressed, and we're getting no pulse from our audience.

Amelia shoots me a beseeching look. Talking about sugar will gets us a heartbeat. The young ones can understand the alchemy in birthday cakes and fresh-baked chocolate chip cookies. I've come to know each of these kids through the shop. Brent, a kid so tall and muscular he's bursting out as a football hero at every seam, is partial to strawberries and cream. His mother insists on the inscription, 'Happy Birthday Sweet Boy!' Tracy has a passion for chocolate so sincere that her cakes are dark as coal, black fudgy cake and solid chocolate ganache. The only colours coming through are the purple flowers I pipe along the perimeter of the cake. Zeke favoured pink on all his birthday cakes up until last year. His allergies are legion and I mark my calendar a month before the day so I have time to find gluten-free, nut-free, and dairy-free recipes that won't send him to the hospital in the middle of his party, no matter what his favourite colour might be.

I'm left breathless knowing that I've baked for every one of these kids and that I actually care about them; me, a woman who never wanted little human creatures of her own, now considering an entire community's children under her watch.

But even though I've reluctantly begun to harbour affection for my Vermont neighbours and their offspring, I don't know if I'm living up to the expectations of that paralysing disembodied voice that held me captive all those years ago. I have a feeling that I'm a lifetime away from living an existence composed of nothing but goodness and kindness. I'm still cranky now and again. While I'm infinitely happier and far better adjusted as a human, I still harbour a bit of the misanthrope in me. But I'm hopeful for my continuing evolution.

I don't know where Ray and I will be when these kids are grown, getting married and celebrating their own children's birthdays. We're thinking of moving on. We're getting older ourselves, old enough to appreciate the value of sleep and of having time to see our families. Our little shop takes every waking moment of our lives, and we're looking to the years when we can enjoy Vermont outside the confines of our store, maybe take our show on the road and explore beyond the Green Mountains with my slightly better attitude toward the world and my unflinching need to bake treats for strangers.

Come to think of it, maybe Saint Nikolaus is looking for an assistant; hell, he's probably eyeing retirement so he can pursue his boyhood dream of being a rock star. I'd happily put on the mantle of my favourite chocolate-pushing saint if he needs a break or even a full-time replacement. Because, looking back at him now, I think I found a kindred spirit on those stairs: slightly bad attitude verging on scary, slovenly attire, and a soft spot for kids and sweets. I think I'd make a half-decent Saint Nikolaus.

* * *

No matter where I land, any kind of future would be dim without the prospect of playing with sugar, butter, and flour. I always want a cookie or a piece of cake to accompany my adventures. And I realise I can honestly say that, yes, baking is my dream job... Had it occurred to me growing up that I might live my adult life dedicated to creating any sweet I desired, I would have considered that to be a future wonderful beyond imagination.

Acknowledgements

I want to thank, with love and an assortment of treats, the beautiful people who tolerate and help me. To my husband, Raymond. You're the best. To my Omi, for having been what an Omi should be. To Sandy for being a one-woman army of love and support. To Dad for loving and encouraging strength in your womenfolk. To Laura Nolan for whipping me into shape and nurturing the book. To Kathleen Finneran, a glorious writer and tremendous teacher. To Cheryl Maisel, who I'd want as a friend in any world: Hollywood, pastry, you name it. To Ann and Anne, writers and friends who possess so much talent and encouragement, you made it impossible for me not to finish. To Larry for being Larry. To Weenie for being a soulmate in dessert and beyond. To our amazing crew at Gesine's and to the best customers...ever. To my family, both stateside and in Germany. To Jesse, Terri & Jeff, Cliff Gilbert-Lurie, Joanne Henderson, Terry Shannon, the Fitzes for digging me out of the snow on a daily basis, the Valentine's Phantom for keeping magic alive, and to the great state of Vermont.

Conversion Charts

Weights

Imperial	Metric
½ oz	10 g
¾ oz	20 g
1 oz	25 g
1½ oz	40 g
2 oz	50 g
2½ oz	60 g
3 oz	75 g
4 oz	110 g
4½ oz	125 g
5 oz	150 g
6 oz	175 g
7 oz	200 g
8 oz	225 g
9 oz	250 g
10 oz	275 g
12 oz	350 g
1 lb	450 g
1 lb 8 oz	700 g
2 lb	900 g
3 lb	1.35 kg

Dimensions

Imperial	Metric
⅛ inch	3 mm
¼ inch	5 mm
½ inch	1 cm
¾ inch	2 cm
1 inch	2.5 cm
1¼ inch	3 cm
1½ inch	4 cm
1¾ inch	4.5 cm
2 inch	5 cm
2½ inch	6 cm
3 inch	7.5 cm
3½ inch	9 cm
4 inch	10 cm
5 inch	13 cm
5¼ inch	13.5 cm
6 inch	15 cm
6½ inch	16 cm
7 inch	18 cm
7½ inch	19 cm
8 inch	20 cm
9 inch	23 cm
9½ inch	24 cm
10 inch	25.5 cm
11 inch	28 cm
12 inch	30 cm

Volume

Imperial	Metric
2 fl oz	55 ml
3 fl oz	75 ml
5 fl oz (¼ pint)	150 ml
10 fl oz (½ pint)	275 ml
1 pint	570 ml
1 ¼ pint	725 ml
1 ¾ pint	1 litre
2 pint	1.2 litre
2½ pint	1.5 litre
4 pint	2.25 litres

Oven Temperatures*

Gas Mark	°F	°C
1	275°F	140°C
2	300°F	150°C
3	325°F	170°C
4	350°F	180°C
5	375°F	190°C
6	400°F	200°C
7	425°F	220°C
8	450°F	230°C
9	475°F	240°C

*Reduce temperatures for fan assisted ovens.

American Cup Conversions

American	Imperial	Metric
1 cup flour	5oz	150g
1 cup caster/ granulated sugar	8oz	225g
1 cup brown sugar	6oz	175g
1 cup butter/margarine/lard	8oz	225g
1 cup sultanas/raisins	7oz	200g
1 cup currants	5oz	150g
1 cup ground almonds	4oz	110g
1 cup golden syrup	12oz	350g
1 cup uncooked rice	7oz	200g
1 cup grated cheese	4oz	110g
1 stick butter	4oz	110g

Liquid Conversions

American	Imperial	Metric
1 tbsp	½ fl oz	15 ml
1/8 cup	1 fl oz	30 ml
¼ cup	2 fl oz	60 ml
½ cup	4 fl oz	120 ml
1 cup	8 fl oz	240 ml
1 pint	16 fl oz	480 ml